# Horse Sense.
# Street Smarts.

## A common-sense collection of quotes about business and life

DON W. HODGES

**Horse Sense. Street Smarts.**

# Contents

# Illustrations

**Horse Sense. Street Smarts.**

**Horse Sense. Street Smarts.**

# Foreword

Our father, Don Hodges, has always been an inspiration to his children and those around him by being a great role model. A man best characterized by his giving heart and unselfish dedication to God, our mother, his children and his clients, Dad has spent his life constantly striving for personal growth. His curiosity and hunger for knowledge has led him to record his personal reflections and thoughts, inspirational messages from countless books and articles, and several axioms by which he has led his life, all of which have been most fortunately bestowed upon us.

The lifelong accumulation of Dad's favorite quotes is listed herein. They are reflections of his beliefs, his positive inspirational outlook, and bits of wisdom. We hope every reader will reflect and enjoy Horse Sense, Street Smarts: a common sense collection of quotes about business and life, by Don Hodges, our loving father.

With admiration and love

*Camille, Craig, and Clark*

The Hodges Family

*December, 2011*

# Preface

The title of this page should read "Collector's Notes" because this project is different than writing a book. It's all about a collection of words of wisdom from a diverse group of individuals. Over 40 years ago I started collecting quotes. Some are by well-known figures from contemporary life, some are from historical figures and some are little known or even unknown. But they have one thing in common; they wrote, spoke or stated ideas that make common sense.

On purpose, I've failed to identify the title or authority of the quotes. Just the name is included. The name is not what is important; their street-smart thoughts are what is being highlighted. The reader may not agree with all of them, but that's not important either. What is important, hopefully, is that the reader will weigh and consider each quote.

This is the type of reading I'd like my own offspring to read and absorb. Nothing would make me happier than to know my own children and grandchildren seriously considered the thoughts in these quotes.

I believe any student, high school or university, can benefit from these potentially life changing words of wisdom. I can assure the reader that some of these thoughts have figured into my own life. They are like "frontlets" as described in the Bible.

One thing I'm absolutely certain about, you'll have a broader and different perspective after reading and cogitating about these jewels of wisdom. Digesting these common sense words can provide the reader, regardless of age, with "Doctorate in Good 'ole Horse Sense."

Best Regards,

Don Hodges

Tim Cox, *Rumbling Thunder*

**Horse Sense. Street Smarts.**

# Acknowledgments

Outside my interest in family and business, I'm a collector and admirer of Western Art. Growing up in West Texas gave me a great appreciation of the western culture with its vast ranches and sturdy farm land. When reviewing choices for visual elements to compliment this book, one of my paintings, by world-renowned artist Tim Cox, stood out as an excellent representation of American business.

Successful business requires many of the skills epitomized by the experienced, salt-of-the-earth cowboy depicted in Tim's *Rumbling Thunder*: providing direction, encouragement, and control to move a herd of strong-willed individuals toward a common goal is the essence of business leadership. That is why I chose this painting for the front cover, and selected other paintings by this talented artist to highlight each chapter.

Tim Cox's depiction of the contemporary west with its glorious skies, rugged cowboys, and hardworking ranchers, the cattle they raise, good horses, and wide open spaces has been giving viewers a thrill for many years. Tim paints what he knows; vibrant cutting horses intent on holding that cow, cowponies covered in sweat after working a hard day, ranch horses sharing a well-earned drink at a glistening water trough.

His cattle have authentic expressions; calves perhaps a little bewildered at a branding, bemused heifers waiting to be fed, a longhorn steer intent on leaving the country, or a herd just shuffling along as they are being driven to better pastures are frequent subjects. Ranchers, cutters, team ropers, or cowhands, all of them touch his heart. Add a striking landscape with dramatic skies; clear blue, wispy pink clouds or spectacular thunderheads and you have a Tim Cox painting.

Tim is especially proud of his 2003 Prix de West Award and his two "Express Ranches Great American Cowboy Awards" from the National Cowboy and Western Heritage Museum. In a 1975 high school English class essay he wrote that one of his fondest wishes was to be a member of the Cowboy Artists of America. His wish was granted in 2007 when he was invited to join the prestigious group. After serving on the Board of Directors and being a member for only a few years, he is currently serving as president for 2011-2012.

**Horse Sense. Street Smarts.**

# Introduction

The topic is business. The authors are the greatest leaders of all time. Their quotes are assembled and presented for your daily insight and inspiration, like vitamins for the mind.

Don Hodges, founder and president of Hodges Capital in Dallas, Texas, shares the wisdom he has collected in over 40 years as an investment advisor and student of business and personal success. As a professional asset manager for institutions, endowments, family offices and individuals, Mr. Hodges has worked with some of most prominent business leaders in America. His book reveals the golden nuggets he has picked up along the way, offering readers the disarming simplicity of common sense in a condensed compendium that certainly merits a place on any executive bookshelf.

Flip through the pages and absorb what Warren Buffett, Ben Franklin, Steve Jobs, Tom Landry, St. Paul, and other great leaders have to say about business ethics, making money, managing people and balancing work, family, church and state. What you gain from a brief glance into this book may very well shape your destiny.

Enjoy *Horse Sense. Street Smarts.* And start weaving this rich collection of common sense into your daily life.

You can bet the ranch on it!

**Horse Sense. Street Smarts.**

# Attitude

**Tim Cox,** *Crossing the Creek*

We've all had circumstances go against us at one time or another. Our luck just seems to run out. When that happens, it's easy to allow a setback to poison us. Our positive attitude runs straight south. Ironically, when things go against us, that's when we need to stay positive more than ever. A positive attitude can actually help us turn the tide.

Whenever a situation brings you to the crossroads of positive or negative, take the positive. It wins every time.

If a man can only have one kind of sense, let him have common sense. If he has that and uncommon sense, he is not far from genius.

*Henry Ward Beecher*

If my mind can conceive it, and my heart can believe it, I know I can achieve it.

*Jesse Jackson*

Whatever your mind can conceive and believe, it can achieve.

*Napoleon Hill*

Joy depends on perspective, not circumstances.

*Robert Jeffress*

Walk on, walk on with hope in your heart and you'll never walk alone.

*Oscar Hammerstein*

Live, love, laugh, and be happy; God's forgiveness is a new beginning.

*John Hagee*

Be the best you can be. Also, be sure to get in quality time with your family.

*Herb Weitzman*

Be not ashamed of mistakes and thus make them crimes.

*Confucius*

Ain't no man can avoid being born average, but there ain't no man got to be common.

*Satchel Paige*

Do what you can, where you are, with what you have.

*Theodore Roosevelt*

**Horse Sense. Street Smarts.**

Your work is going to fill a large part of your life, and the only way to be truly satisfied is to do what you believe is great work, and the only way to do great work is to love what you do. If you haven't found it yet keep looking. Don't settle. As with matters of the heart, you'll know when you find it, and like any great relationship it just gets better as the years roll on. So keep looking until you find it. Don't settle

*Steve Jobs*

Hurting people hurt people. Hurting people get hurt more than others.

*Mac Brunson*

Get all the education you can, but then, by God, do something. Don't just stand there, make it happen.

*Lee Iacocca*

Difficult people are the sand paper needed to smooth you out.

*Mac Brunson*

I believe that the moment I tell myself 'I've had a full and satisfying life,' that will be the end. No matter how old I get, I intend always to embrace the future. It's the same with a company as with people: turn back and it's all over. You've got to look the future in the eye and step straight ahead.

*Eiji Toyoda*

When in doubt, make it stout.

*David Adickes*

Live your life with no secrets.

*Trammell Crow*

It's how you bounce back from the lowest point that makes you who you are.

*Karen Cremmins Herrera*

I dropped my habits of immediately contradicting other people and pushing hard for my opinions. Rather, I stopped arguing my side and started asking questions instead.

*Ben Franklin*

How old would you be if you didn't know how old you was?

*Satchell Paige*

Build your dreams and your dreams will build you.

*Dr. Robert Schuller*

Whatever you do in life do it with gusto and have fun.

*Trent Lott*

Sign on to a cause because you believe in it and then pledge with passion—that you will make a positive difference each day on behalf of it.

*Colleen Barrett*

Do something for someone every day.

*Maurice Acers*

If anything terrifies me, I must try to conquer it.

*Francis Charles Chicester*

First, sort out what you believe in—you then apply it. You don't compromise on things that matter

*Margaret Thatcher*

Our vision controls the way we think and, therefore, the way we act. The vision we have of our jobs determines what we do and the opportunities we see or don't see.

*Charles Koch*

If you don't make mistakes, you can't make decisions. You can't dwell on them.

*Warren Buffett*

**Horse Sense. Street Smarts.**

Courage is being able to manage fear.

*Rudy Giulani*

Nature has decreed that extreme sameness of thinking provides its own self-correcting mechanism.

*Street Smart Investor*

Nobody can be as persuasive as one who's not hampered by the facts or truth.

*Anonymous*

Charles Darwin used to say that whenever he ran into something that contradicted a conclusion he cherished, he was obliged to write the new finding down within 30 minutes. Otherwise his mind would work to reject the discordant information, much as the body rejects transplants.

*Warren Buffett*

Life's battles don't always go to the stronger or faster man; but soon or late the man who wins is the man who thinks he can.

*Anonymous*

What lies behind us and what lies before us are tiny matters compared to what lies within us.

*Oliver Wendell Holmes*

Always follow your heart and your passions.

*Colleen Barrett*

The quality of a person's life is indirectly proportionate to their commitment to excellence, regardless of their chosen field of endeavor.

*Vincent T. Lombardi*

If you expect perfection from people, your whole life is a series of disappointments, grumblings and complaints. If, on the contrary, you pitch your expectations low, taking folks as the inefficient creatures which they are, you are frequently surprised by having them perform better than you had hoped.

Bruce Barton

### Risk Taking is Freedom

To laugh is to risk appearing the fool.

To weep is to risk appearing sentimental

To reach out for another is to risk involvement.

To expose feelings is to risk exposing your true self.

To place your ideas, your dreams before the crowd, is to risk their loss.

To love is to risk not being loved in return.

To live is to risk dying.

To hope is to risk despair.

To try is to risk failure.

But risk must be taken because the greatest hazard in life is to risk nothing.

The person who risks nothing does nothing, has nothing, and is nothing.

He may avoid suffering and sorrow, but he simply cannot learn, feel, change, grow, love, live.

Chained by his certitudes, he is a slave, he has forfeited freedom.

Only a person who risks is free.

Anonymous

A man is tested by his reaction to man's praise.

Proverbs 27:2

Fear and the emotions that come from its being do more to paralyze useful effort, good work, and finely thought-out plans, than aught else known to man. It is the hobgoblin of the race. It has ruined the lives of thousands of people. It has destroyed the finely budding characters of men and women, and made negative individuals of them in the place of strong, reliant, courageous doers of useful things.

Worry is the oldest child of Fear. It settles down upon one's mind, and crowds out all of the developing good things to be found there. Like the cuckoo in the sparrow's nest, it destroys the rightful occupants of the mind. Laid there as an egg by its parent, Fear, Worry soon hatches out and begins to make trouble.

In place of the cheerful and positive 'I can and I will' harmony, Worry beings to rasp out in raucous tones: 'Supposin,' 'What if,' 'But,' 'I can't,' 'I'm unlucky,' 'I never could do things right,' 'Things never turn out right with me,' and so on until all the minor notes have been sounded. It makes one sick bodily and inert mentally. It retards one's progress and is a constant stumbling block in our path upward.

*Richard D. Wyckoff*

There is not a worry in the world worth worrying about.

*Connie Mack*

On recovering from disappointment: It's no use sitting upon me, for I am India rubber—and I bounce.

*Winston Churchill*

Believing in yourself is a vital ingredient in determining your success. Every achievement, big or small, begins in your mind. It starts as a thought. Your self-image comes into play as you act on that thought. Confidence stimulates your ability to perform.

*Mary Kay Ash*

Youth is not a time of life—it's a state of mind: it is a temper of the will, a quality of the imagination, a vigor of the emotions, a predominance of courage over timidity, of the appetite for adventure over love of ease. Nobody grows old by merely living a number of years; people grow old only by deserting their ideals. Years wrinkle the skin, but to give up enthusiasm wrinkles the soul. Worry, doubt, self-distrust, fear, & despair—these are the long, long years that bow the head & turn the growing spirit back to dust. Whether seventy or sixteen, there is in every being's heart the love of wonder, the sweet amazement at the start & the star-like things & thought, the undaunted challenge of events, the unfailing childlike appetite for what next, & the joy & the game of life. You are as young as your faith, as old as your doubt; as young as your self-confidence, as old as your fear; as young as your hope, as old as your despair. So long as your heart receives messages of beauty, cheer, courage, grandeur, & power from the earth, from man & from the Infinite, so long are you young. When the wires are all down & all the central place of your heart is covered with the snows of pessimism & the ice of cynicism, then you are grown old indeed & may God have mercy on your soul.

*Gen. Douglas MacArthur*

Lead by example.

*Kevin McGuire*

I never look back to see what I could do or might have done differently. I guess I'm a total pragmatist. I can't relive my life, not for one minute, so why reflect on that instead of thinking about today and tomorrow? Each day I do the best I can and move on. I also learn from lessons of the past by improving on the present and future. What good are regrets? Regrets slow you down. Regrets cause you to fail to pay attention to the future. So I never log, count or inventory my regrets. I move on.

*Colin Powell*

The longer I live, the more I realize the impact of attitude on life. Attitude, to me, is more important than facts. It is more important than the past, than education, than money, than circumstances, than failures, than success, than what other people think or say or do. It is more important than appearance, giftedness or skill. It will make or break a company...a church...a home. The remarkable thing is we have a choice every day regarding the attitude we will embrace for that day. We cannot change our past. We cannot change the fact that people will act in a certain way. We cannot change the inevitable. The only thing we can do is play on the one string we have, and that is our attitude. I am convinced that life is 10% what happens to me and 90% how I react to it. And so it is with you...we are in charge of our attitudes.

*Charles Swindoll*

Feed yourself positive thoughts; you can do positive things. Feed yourself negative thoughts; you do negative things.

*Dr. Robert Schuller*

I once read a silly fairy tale, called The Three Princes of Serendip: as their Highnesses travelled, they were always making discoveries, by accident and sagacity, of things which they were not in quest of. Serendipity is defined as the gift of finding, by chance and by sagacity, valuable or agreeable things not sought for. It is not an 'either/or' phenomenon, but both accident and sagacity have to come in while one is in the pursuit of something else. Thus 'accidental discovery' is not a synonym for serendipity. In other words, discoveries (or opportunities) occur when you are looking for something with your eyes wide open.

*Stanley Marcus*

Everybody talks about wanting to change things and help and fix, but ultimately all you can do is fix yourself. And that's a lot. Because if you can fix yourself, it has a ripple effect.

*Rob Reiner*

We do not inherit the world, we create it. We shape our fate and the world—by the choices we make, the actions we take, and the way we decide to live our lives.

*C. Fred Kleinknecht*

Fame is a vapor, Popularity an accident, Riches take wings. Those who cheer today, condemn tomorrow. One thing only endures—Character.

*Horace Greeley*

Opportunity is not a lengthy visitor.

*Anonymous*

A winner never quits and a quitter never wins.

*Vince Lombardi*

Character is not something you have; it is something that inevitably shows itself in what you do. It is determined by stories of which you are a part. Character is values lived. Every thought is rooted in value; every value requires a choice; every choice defines a character. The more we are conscious of our role as characters and the more we purposefully choose the stories by which we live, the healthier we will be. Character is not something you have; it is something you are that inevitably shows itself in what you do.

*Dr. Daniel Taylor*

Honesty is like a powerful drug. It needs to be taken in small doses. I have said things that were true and just screamed to be said. But that should not be the test. It also should be helpful and constructive.

*Phil Gramm*

A leader has to be strong enough to make his own decisions and stick to them, even when they're unpopular. Conversely, a great leader isn't pigheaded enough to stick with a bad choice. He must be self-confident enough to solicit opinions and change his mind without worrying that he'll appear weak.

*Rudy Giuliani*

Character is much easier kept than recovered.

*Thomas Paine*

Sarah and I live on the east side of our mountain. It is the sunrise side, not the sunset side. It is the side to see the day that is coming, not the side to see the day that is gone. The best day is the day coming.

*Tom Lea*

**Horse Sense. Street Smarts.**

I think the distinguishing thing in a leader is integrity, the ability to earn trust.

*Roger Staubach*

It's how you think that makes you successful. If you have a positive attitude, good things will happen.

*Tom Landry*

You got to be careful if you don't know where you're going, because you might not get there.

*Yogi Berra*

A lifetime of investment research has taught me to become more and more humble about making predictions.

*Sir John Templeton*

It's easy to grin when your ship comes in, and you've got the stock market beat. But the man who's worthwhile is the man who can smile when his shorts are too tight in the seat.

*Blackie Sherrod*

The only safe thing is to take a chance.

*Mike Nichols*

Don't talk about your ailments...remember what's important in life: faith, family and friends. Tolerance, in fact, is the most important human quality. Learn something new this year and try a new adventure.

Quit making excuses and get involved. Spend quality time with children and grandchildren. Children and grandchildren must come first. Be a good neighbor. Don't wait for a big cause...perform some community service.

*Barbara Bush*

Do all the good you can, by all the means you can, in all the ways you can, in all the places you can, at all the times you can, to all the people you can, as long as ever you can.

*John Wesley*

Fire the planners. Hire the freaks.

Nobody gives you power. You just take it.

Meet too much, accomplish too little.

You've got a new boss. Buy a mirror: it's you.

*Tom Peters*

No matter where you learn your values—in business, in the military, in life itself—your values do matter.

*George H. W. Bush*

It is a good thing to have all the props pulled out from under us occasionally. It gives us some sense of what is rock under our feet, and what is sand. It stops us from taking anything for granted.

*Madeleine L'Engle*

It's always easier to get into debt than out of debt! It's always easier to borrow than to pay it back. It's always easier to get into a partnership than to get out of one. Falling in love (infatuation) is easy—the difficult part is staying in love. It's always easier to fill your schedule than to fulfill it. You can get so many irons in the fire that you put out the fire. The person who burns the candle at both ends is not as bright as he thinks he is.

*Anonymous author*

You make your own luck.

*Lance Armstrong*

Failure? I have never encountered it, only temporary setbacks.

*Bill Marriott*

**Horse Sense. Street Smarts.**

Don't ever let somebody tell you, you shouldn't try something out because it won't work.

*Wilson Greatbatch*

To others, being wrong is a source of shame; to me, recognizing my mistakes is a source of pride. Once we realize that imperfect understanding is the human condition, there is no shame in being wrong, only in failing to correct our mistakes.

*George Soros*

You can't plan life, life plans you. If you stay flexible and roll with it, you can survive. Every time I make a mistake, I learn something. The secret is to never stop learning.

*Tony Bennett*

From playing ball, I learned about competitiveness. It taught me both how to win and it taught me how to lose. I prefer to win and make every effort to win.

*Dr. Denton Cooley*

Do what is right, not what you think the high headquarters wants or what you think will make you look good.

*Gen. Norman Schwarzkopf*

Just get off your behind and do it. It doesn't matter if you didn't do it right, because not doing it at all is definitely not doing it right.

*Mark Spitz*

You cannot carry what did or did not happen from one day to the next, especially if it's negative, into something that's supposed to be a positive experience for the next day.

*Mark Spitz*

Eighty percent of things that happen in your life are irrelevant and twenty percent of things that happen in your life are relevant. I've tried to focus my time and energy on that 20%.

*Don Tomnitz*

I've always understood that courage is about the management of fear, not the absence of fear.

*Rudy Giuliani*

Courage is doing what you have to do even though you are afraid.

*Rudy Giuliani*

In a crisis, when everybody else gets very, very excited, you have to become the calmest person in the room, so you can figure a way out of the situation.

*Rudy Giuliani*

I love the challenge of doing things people say can't be done. The minute somebody says, 'That can't be done,' I respond by thinking it would be interesting, exciting and fulfilling to prove it can be done.

*Rudy Giuliani*

Rate everything on a scale of one to five: a one being you stumped your toe; a five being you get your left arm cut off. Measure everything that happens to you against that scale. You'll see that not many things that happen are particularly bad.

*Grant Jackson*

It isn't the size of the man in the fight; it is the size of the fight in the man.

*Said about Bob Fitzsimmons, boxer*

To play the game is great...to win the game is greater... but to love the game is the greatest of all.

*Anonymous*

Manners are a sensitive awareness of the feelings of others. If you have that awareness, you have good manners, no matter which fork you use.

*Emily Post*

**Horse Sense. Street Smarts.**

It is that the influence of a really good person lives on in the benefits he confers upon others, and that influence never really fades. Courage and integrity are among the most valuable virtues of humanity outlasting even death itself.

*Dr. Ashley Montague*

The truth is cancer is the best thing that ever happened to me. Don't know why I got the illness, but it did wonders for me, and I wouldn't want to walk away from it. Why would I want to change, even for a day, the most important and shaping event in my life?

*Lance Armstrong*

The longer the press is on the site, the more they will convince themselves that the underdog will win.

*Harry Grayson*
*(Remarking at the Harris-Patterson title fight)*

It's what you learn after you know it all that counts.

*Earl Weaver*

Nothing gives one person so great an advantage over another as to remain cool and unruffled under all circumstances.

*Thomas Jefferson*

When one door closes, another door opens; but we often look so long and so regretfully upon the closed door that we do not see the ones which open for us.

*Alexander Graham Bell*

A sense of humor is part of the art of leadership, of getting along with people, of getting things done.

*Dwight Eisenhower*

The negative principle negates. The positive principle creates. The negative principle doubts. The positive principle believes. The negative principle accepts defeat. The positive principle goes for victory.

*Norman Vincent Peale*

My parents taught me that character never quits, and with character, patience and persistence, dreams can be realized.

*Pete Maravich*

All of us need to pause every now and then to examine where the rush of the world and our own activities are taking us.

*Bernard Baruch*

I've never lost a game. Some just ended too soon.

*Bobby Layne*

Don't find fault. Find a remedy.

*Henry Ford*

Don't hurry, don't worry. You're only here for a short visit. So don't forget to stop and smell the roses.

*Walter Hagen*

I'll lay me down to bleed awhile. Though I am wounded, I am not slain. I shall rise and fight again.

*English Ballad*

The basic flaw of the Titanic was not technical but the attitude of mind which affected all who had anything to do with her—an unswerving faith in progress, industry and science.

*Michael Davie*

You're not beaten until you give up.

*Herschel Walker*

Panic breeds faster than confidence.

*Bill Stransby*

If you think you can do a thing or think you can't do a thing, you're right.

*Henry Ford*

Most people are too confrontational. If you start by arguing, it intensifies others' desires to prove they are right.

*Morey Stettner*

Be cheerful. Strive to be happy.

*Max Ehrmann*

Don't judge each day by the harvest you reap but by the seeds you sow.

*Robert Louis Stevenson*

We've got to find a way to laugh at the things that are getting us down. A few days after 9/11, I noticed that there was a lot of activity in New York. People in restaurants were laughing and talking. I wondered if it hadn't hit them what really happened. But then I realized that they were expressing that life goes on.

*Steve Martin*

Dance like no one is watching, love like you'll never be hurt, sing like no one is listening, live like it's heaven on earth.

*William Purkey*

How you see yourself is the way you'll end up being.

*Kenneth Cole*

Life is too short to wake up in the morning with regrets, so love the people who treat you right. Forgive the ones who don't. Life is 10% what you make of it and 90% how you take it.

*Tony Lisotta*

Believe you will be successful and you will

*Dale Carnegie*

I never quit trying; I never felt that I didn't have a chance to win.

*Arnold Palmer*

The real beginning of being happy is having gratitude.

*Cameron Diaz*

If you go through life convinced that your way is always the best,-all the new ideas in the world will pass you by.

*Akio Morita*

Life is full of twists and turns and difficult times—it's how we handle them that matters.

*Sally Swanson*

Breaking the habit of self-criticism can pay big dividends in mental and physical health. The way you see yourself can be challenged and changed, and it can literally create new neural pathways in your brain. As your thinking improves, your immune system improves, your digestion is better, you don't compensate by overeating or drinking, and your anxiety levels go down.

*Dr. Robert Leahy*

In a way you're writing your own obit every day. You're making the lead paragraph positive and constructive or not. Someone's going to sum you up one day. You want to live your professional life in a way that they can write good things.

*Peggy Noonan*

People who are depressed tend to believe that's just the way they are. Instead of viewing yourself as a failed end product, think of yourself as a temporarily derailed work in progress.

*Joe Kita*

The richest man in town is the one who has his health.

*Jerry Crabb*

Walking into a room or meeting carrying frustration and disappointment brings everyone down. Better to be positive about what you and they can be thankful for in your work and life. If you take a glass of water and add ice, the water gets colder. Likewise, it gets warmer if you add something hot. You have the same effect on the mood and energy of every room you enter.

*Noah Blumenthal*

The way to get ahead is to over-deliver. Expand the organization's expectations of you and exceed them.

*Jack Welch*

Managing is like holding a dove in your hand. If you hold it too tightly, you kill it, but if you hold it too loosely, you lose it.

*Tommy Lasorda*

Don't brag about yourself—let others praise you.

*Proverbs 27: 20*

Don't be happy to see your enemies trip and fall down.

*Proverbs 24:17*

Don't be a fool and quickly lose your temper—be sensible and patient.

*Proverbs 29:11*

Too much pride causes trouble.

*Proverbs 13:10*

What did it for me? It wasn't my education or experience. It was my passion.

*Andrea Jung*

I don't accept losing.

*Dick Strong*

Winners are people who have fun and produce results as a result of their zest.

*Tom Peters*

If you play to win, the game never ends.

*Stan Mikita*

It's hard for me to lead anybody until I've shown them how I work, prepare and practice. If I even want to lead anybody, the first thing I have to do is to set an example by earning their respect.

*Kurt Warner*

Don't ever tell a lie or say to someone, I'll get even with you!

*Proverbs 24:29*

Pride leads to destruction; humility leads to honor.

*Proverbs 18:12*

Stay humble, get better.

*Mark Ingram, Sr.*

Show class, have pride, and display character.

*Paul "Bear" Bryant*

I want to do it because I want to do it.

*Amelia Earhart*

Do all you can for everyone who deserves your help. Don't tell your neighbor to come back tomorrow, if you can help today.

*Proverbs 3:27—28*

I come to every situation not with my knowledge, but with my ignorance, and I ask questions.

*Peter Drucker*

Remember to always treat the little people right.

*William H. Atkinson*

It is always important to make a positive first impression with a firm handshake and good eye contact.

*Dr. L. Jack Bolton*

**Horse Sense. Street Smarts.**

Only you know when you look in the mirror if you gave it your best shot. As long as you did that, you have to turn the page and get on with your life.

*Rocky Marciano*

When you fail, it's ok to get depressed, cry, and blame others for awhile. Eventually, you have to get over it and move on.

*Jamie Dimon*

Begin with the end in mind.

*Norman Brinker*

The fact that I have had a tragic event in life shouldn't change it.

*Brian Burke*

The happiest people don't necessarily have the best of. everything; they just make the best of everything they have.

*Anonymous*

Loneliness can be transmitted. Loneliness is not just the property of an individual. It can be transmitted across people. People who become lonely eventually move to the periphery of their social network, becoming increasingly isolated, which can exacerbate their loneliness and affect social connectedness.

*John Cacioppo*

You marry to the level of your self-esteem.

*Marie Osmond*

What makes a king out of a slave? Courage.

*The Cowardly Lion (Wizard of Oz)*

If we go into the mine with fear, we can work, but if we work with fear, it's better not to go in at all. A fearful miner is accident prone and could injure someone else.

*Omar Reygadas*

To fail to be civil to someone—to treat them harshly, rudely, or condescendingly—is not only bad manners, it also, and more ominously, signals a disdain or contempt for them as moral beings.

*Richard Boyd*

Confidence, which is the antithesis of uncertainty, is the most important factor when it comes to the economy and the stock market.

*Bill Deener*

People who believe in the power of talent tend not to fulfill their potential because they're so concerned with looking smart and not making mistakes. But people who believe that talent can be developed are the ones who really push, stretch, confront their own mistakes, and learn from them.

*Anonymous*

Three things in human life are important. The first is to be kind. The second is to be kind. And the third is to be kind.

*Henry James*

It is a helpful habit for a businessman to be optimistic and enthusiastic. It will make his own work better and easier and will also serve to hearken and inspire others.

*J. Paul Getty*

Never say or do anything when you are angry.

*Herman Pistor*

Don't be afraid to leave your comfort zone.

*Dunia Shive*

I have learned to be a realist, see it the way it is, not the way you want to see it.

*Robert Nardelli*

**Horse Sense. Street Smarts.**

I understand aspiration. I like people who want to succeed and admire people who do.

*Tony Blair*

The most polite and gentlemanly treatment of all customers, however insignificant in their business, is insisted upon. Proper respect must be shown to all – let them be men, women, or children, rich or poor – it must not be forgotten that this company is dependent on these same people for its business.

*Henry Wells*

There's no such thing as bad weather, just different kinds of good weather.

*Col. Harlan Sanders*

We can't all be rich, we can't all be beautiful, but we can all be gracious.

*Mrs. Schonfelder*

About dancing in the end zone after scoring: Show a little class; act like you've been there before.

*Emmitt Smith, Jr.*

Anything can happen if you let it.

*Mary Poppins*

I don't care how much you know, tell me how much you care.

*Malouf Abraham, Jr.*

The people who have helped me most in my career told me things I did not want to hear the fist time I heard them.

*Romil Bahl*

Pay obsessive attention to each customer.

*Bruce Brookshire*

Keep calm and carry on.

*Winston Churchill*

There will be be somebody with more than you and somebody with less than you. So you might as well be satisfied.

*Melba Roeckeman*

Christ meant for his followers to be different. But being different was not enough. They were to be the cleanest, kindest, most unselfish, friendliest, most courteous, most industrious, most thoughtful, truest and the most loving people on earth.

*Billy Graham*

As you wander through this life, my friend, no matter what your goal, keep your eye upon the donut and not upon the hole.

*Malouf Abraham, Sr.*

## Desiderata

Go placidly amid the noise and the haste, and remember what peace there may be in silence. As far as possible, without surrender, be on good terms with all persons. Speak your truth quietly and clearly; and listen to others, even to the dull and the ignorant, they, too, have their story. Avoid loud and aggressive persons; they are vexations to the spirit.

If you compare yourself to others, you may become vain and bitter; for always there will be greater and lesser persons than yourself.

Enjoy your achievements as well as your plans. Keep interested in your own career, however humble; it is a real possession in the changing fortunes of time.

Exercise caution in your business affairs, for the world is full of trickery. But let not this blind you to what virtue there is; many persons strive for high ideals, and everywhere life is full of heroism.

Be yourself. Especially do not feign affection. Neither be cynical about love; for in the face of all aridity and disenchantment it is as

**Horse Sense. Street Smarts.**

perennial as the grass. Take kindly the counsel of the years, gracefully surrendering the things of youth.

Nurture strength of spirit to shield you in sudden misfortune. But do not distress yourself with dark imaginings. Many fears are born of fatigue and loneliness.

Beyond a wholesome discipline, be gentle with yourself. You are a child of the universe, no less than the trees and the stars; you have a right to be here. And whether or not it is clear to you, no doubt the universe is unfolding as it should.

Therefore, be at peace with God, whatever you conceive him to be, and whatever your labors and aspirations in the noisy confusion of life, keep peace in your soul. With all its sham drudgery and broken dreams; it is still a beautiful world.

*Max Ehrmann*

When you walk through a storm
Keep your chin up high
And don't be afraid of the dark.
At the end of the storm
Is a golden sky
And the sweet silver song of a lark.

Walk on through the wind,
Walk on through the rain,
Tho' your dreams be tossed and blown.
Walk on, walk on, with hope in your heart
And you'll never walk alone,
You'll never walk alone.

*Oscar Hammerstein*

Only when you decide when enough is enough – then you can run your life and your contributions very easily.

*Jim Waterfield*

Make it happen.

*Robert Hodges*

I'm doing what I want to do, and I'm on the road I like being on. But I like to keep that road open so I can go to the left or the right. I want to keep the adventure alive.

*Dan Beck*

Don't be looking too far ahead. Live in the moment.

*Linda Davis*

Relationships are built one at a time, not mass produced.

*Wayne Jordan*

I'm not going to worry about what's going to happen two days from now, or I'd be unhappy today.

*Ken Langone*

Don't ever take a job for the title or the paycheck. Take it if you have a passion for it.

*Colleen Barrett*

Always focus on your clients and your teams: take good care of them and everything will work out.

*Ross Perot*

Hiring managers don't actually want to hear about you in interviews–they want to hear what you can do for them. The same goes for potential clients. Get out of your own head and get into theirs.

*Ramit Sethi*

Sometimes a bad analogy can get in the way of a good argument.

*Steve Schwarzman*

Fits of depression come over most of us. Usually cheerful as we may be, we must at intervals be cast down. The strong are not always vigorous; the wise, not always ready; the brave, not always courageous; and the joyous, not always happy. There may be here and there men of iron...but surely the rust frets even these.

*Charles Spurgeon*

**Horse Sense. Street Smarts.**

# Realism

**Tim Cox,** *Thunder Rolls*

Every human being is capable of conning themselves. There are times we want something so badly that we convince ourselves we can have it. A lack of realism can get us into trouble. Do not just see what YOU want to see. Seek advice. Instead of saying, "To thine own self be true," say "To thine own self be honest." Keep an open mind. Being honest with ourselves is the key to realism.

There is nothing to fear from truth. Being truthful is essential to being an independent thinker and obtaining greater understanding of what is right.

*Ray Dalio*

Never say anything about a person you wouldn't say to him directly. If you do, you are a slimy weasel.

*Ray Dalio*

Your character is what you really are; your reputation is merely what people think you are.

*John Wooden*

There's just no way can we always make the right decision; that doesn't mean you're an idiot. But it does mean you must focus on how serious the consequence could be if you turn out to be wrong,

*Peter Bernstein*

When life looks like Easy Street, there's danger at your door.

*Tim Ballard*

Things men have made with wakened hands, and put soft life into, are awake through years with transferred touch, and go on glowing for long years. And for this reason, some old things are lovely— warm still with the life of forgotten men who made them.

*D. H. Lawrence*

Getting along doesn't have to mean going along. You don't have to be a 'yes' man. Just do your best and be honest with yourself and with others.

*Benny Carter*

There's a big difference between doing something that turns out to be wrong and doing something that is wrong.

*Norman Gin*

**Horse Sense. Street Smarts.**

The price to stay is equal to or greater than the price to get here.

*Larry Foster*

Those who cannot remember the past are condemned to repeat it.

*George Santayana*

If you're fortunate enough to have curiosity, my best advice is to follow your curiosity.

*Wilson Greatbatch*

Experience can tell you what not to do, but not what to do.

*Dr. Vladimir Rockov*

Unless you change direction, you are likely to arrive at where you are headed.

*Chinese proverb*

Failing to plan is planning to fail.

*Ben Franklin*

We do not need more material development; we need more spiritual development. We do not need more intellectual power; we need more moral power. We do not need more knowledge; we need more character. We do not need more government; we need more culture. We do not need more law; we need more religion. We do not need more of the things that are seen; we need more of the things that are unseen.

*Calvin Coolidge*

A teacher affects eternity; he can never tell where his influence stops.

*Henry Adams*

The most important thing in life is to learn how to give out love, and let it come in.

*Morrie Schwartz*

Love is how you stay alive, even after you are gone.

*Morrie Schwartz*

What can we lose? The worst that can happen is that he'll refuse.

*Oscar Hammerstein*

Isn't it common sense, that if you're going to learn something, you go to the masters?

*Tony Bennett*

Concentration is the secret of strength in politics, in war, in trade; in short, in all management of human affairs.

*Ralph Waldo Emerson*

Only those are fit to live who do not fear to die. And none are fit to die who have shrunk from the joy of life and the duty of life. Both life and death are parts of the same Great Adventure.

*Theodore Roosevelt*

The eye nor the intellect knows what the heart sees.

*Anonymous*

I think we must agree that all a man can do is beat the people who are around at the same time he is. He cannot win from those who came before, any more that he can from those who may come afterward. It is grossly unfair to anyone who takes pride in the record he is able to compile, that he must see it compared to those of other players who have been competing against entirely different people under wholly different conditions.

*Bobby Jones*

Partial truth is the enemy's biggest weapon.

*Ross McKnight*

**Horse Sense. Street Smarts.**

On passing from a free country into one which is not free, the traveler is struck by the change. In the former, all is bustle and activity; in the latter, everything seems calm and motionless.

*Alexis de Tocqueville*

The only thing we have to fear is fear itself, nameless unreasoning unjustified terror, which paralyzes needed efforts to convert retreat into advance.

*Franklin D. Roosevelt*

No one is so cocky as the one who doesn't know what he doesn't know.

*Richard C. Halverson*

Life can only be understood backwards, but has to be lived forwards.

*Soren Kierkegaard*

Some parents make their children believe that whatever happens is so crucial, and it really isn't. Children's lives are not determined in their 10th year or 15th year or by whether they get into the right college or have one bad year in school. I think too much pressure is put on lads to be perfect.

*Rudy Giuliani*

Don't form an opinion about an important matter until you've heard all the relevant facts and arguments, or until circumstances force you to form an opinion without recourse to all the facts.

*Steven Sample*

The right thing to do is usually the hardest thing to do.

*Larry Waterhouse*

When the legends die, the dreams end. When the dreams die, there is no more greatness.

*Korczak Ziolkowski*

Luck is the residue of design.

*Branch Rickey*

If you visit the city where you were born you live longer.

*Oz Tangun*

Is it new or is it new to you?

*Alex Paris*

You don't know where you are going until you know where you have come from.

*Patrick Henry*

The tide moves all boats whether an ocean liner or garbage barge.

*Arthur Cashen*

You are neither right nor wrong because people agree with you.

*Warren Buffet*

You can only build on what your mother and father taught you, what you learned in school and what you've taught yourself. It's the basic foundation you have that you're building on.

*Rudy Giuliani*

The doughnut has a hole in the middle. If there wasn't a hole, it wouldn't be a doughnut. The nothingness of the center creates the somethingness of the doughnut.

*Scott Livengood*

There are some problems that can't be solved. They must be managed.

*Gen. Charles de Gaulle*

Learn the difference between the ants and the elephants.

*Tom Kirk*

You can't pay back—you can only pay forward.

*Woody Hayes*

Ninety percent of each battle is information.

*Napoleon*

The first wealth is health.

*Ralph Waldo Emerson*

Half truths are much more deceptive than outright lies.

*Bill Bright*

Discovery consists of seeing what everyone has seen, and thinking what nobody has thought.

*Albert Szent-Györgyi*

To know, and not to act, is not to know.

*Wang Yangming*

Genius has to do with believing your own thoughts.

*Ralph Waldo Emerson*

There is no authority except facts. Facts are obtained by accurate observation. Deductions are to be made only from facts.

*William Boeing*

The difference between a loser and a disastrous loser is that the loser can still make money.

*Ned Davis*

That what is most feared is least likely to occur.

*Dessauer's Journal*

'When sentiment is negative, you can always find a few clouds on the horizon.

*Norman G. Fosback*

Everything is possible to him who dares

*A. G. Spalding*

It isn't what we don't know that gives us trouble. It's what we know that ain't so.

*Will Rogers*

"You can buy a man's time; you can buy his physical presence at a given place; you can even buy a measured number of his skilled, muscular motions per hour, but, you cannot buy enthusiasm, you cannot buy loyalty, you cannot buy the devotion of hearts, minds, or souls. These you must earn.

*Clarence Francis*

A mind that is stretched by a new idea never returns to its original dimensions.

*Oliver Wendell Holmes*

Property is the fruit of labor—property is desirable—it is a positive good in the world. That some should be rich, shows that others may become rich, and hence is an encouragement to industry and enterprise. Let not him who is houseless put down the house of another, but let him labor diligently and build one for himself, thus by example assuring that his own shall be safe from violence when built.

*Abraham Lincoln*

You have to follow your brain when it tells you to do something.

*Granville Lassater*

Vision is the ability to see the invisible

*Jonathan Swift*

Seek first to understand, and then to be understood.

*Anonymous*

What everybody knows isn't worth knowing.

*Anonymous*

**Horse Sense. Street Smarts.**

He who is not liberal in his youth, has no heart; he who is not conservative in his maturity has no brain.

*Old French Proverb*

The young man knows the rules. The old man knows the exceptions.

*Anonymous*

An error is not a mistake until one fails to correct it.

*Anonymous*

To sin by silence when you should speak out makes cowards of all men.

*Voltaire*

Forecasting is always risky business, particularly if it happens to be about the future.

*Sam Goldwyn*

The simple problem of our age is how to act decisively in the absence of certainty.

*Bertrand Russell*

Pay attention to small things and do not let them get out of control.

*Rudy Giuliani*

We should be careful to get out of an experience only the wisdom that was in it—and stop there, lest we be like the cat that sits on a hot stove-lid. She will never sit down on a hot stove-lid again—and that is well, but also she will never sit down on a cold one anymore.

*Mark Twain*

The simple problem of our age is how to act decisively in the absence of certainty.

*Bertrand Russell*

Be fearful when others are greedy and greedy when others are fearful.

*Warren Buffett*

**Realism**

The four stages of life: Believe in Santa Claus. Don't believe in Santa Claus. You are Santa Claus. You look like Santa Claus

*Anonymous*

As Jack Lemmon used to tell me, If you've done well, it's your responsibility to send the elevator back down.

*Kevin Spacey*

Trust everyone, but cut the cards.

*Ronald Reagan*

It takes 20 years to build a reputation and five minutes to ruin it.

*Warren Buffet*

A good name is better than money.

*Joe Louis' Mother*

Conveniently leaving out information is just as unethical as purposely omitting information.

*Ohley Myers*

To create the future is to be the enemy of today.

*Peter Drucker*

Your memory works if you keep using it. Keep learning trying to remember things

*Norman Lloyd*

Never suffer an exception to occur till the new habit is securely rooted in your life.

*William James*

A name is made up of little promises kept to the letter. It is made up of faithfulness, loyalty, honesty, of efficiency in your work. In short, a name is the blueprint of the thing we call character. You ask, 'What's in a name?' I answer, 'Just about everything you do.'

*The Jewish Press*

Always buy art of the first quality, as it will do much better than second quality works.

*Rudolf Wunderlich*

Ideas reach their greatest popularity and broadest distribution when they have become irrelevant, obsolete or downright dangerous.

*Scott Burns*

To educate a man in mind and not in morals is to educate a menace to society.

*Theodore Roosevelt*

The unexpected happens. You had better prepare for it.

*Margaret Thatcher*

There is no better way to clarify your own thinking than to try to explain it to someone else.

*Margaret Thatcher*

There's no one who can give you wisdom. You have to obtain it yourself and mold it to your own person.

*Chuck Yeager*

When everyone thinks alike, everyone is likely to be wrong.

*Humphrey Neill*

You don't have to be rich and you don't have to be famous, but for your own sake, just don't be ordinary.

*Jack Roach*

Science is not quick—it means floundering a lot.

*John Bachrus*

People are habitually guided by the rear-view mirror and, for the most part, by the vistas immediately behind them.

*Warren Buffett*

The most important thing in communication is to hear what isn't being said.

*Peter Drucker*

Britain's three main foes in World War I: Germans, Austrians, and Drink. As far as I can see, the greatest of the foes is Drink.

*David Lloyd George*

Watch your thoughts, they become words. Watch your words, they become your actions. Watch your actions, they become habits. Watch your habits, they become character. Watch your character, it becomes your destiny.

*Winston Churchill*

The naked truth is always better than the best-dressed lie.

*Ann Landers*

Reformers tend to preach to the converted, sparing themselves the harsh observations of critics. You can't be sure you're right until you know the other fellow's argument better than he does.

*Milton Friedman*

Try to read the handwriting on the wall, even though it may be confusing or contradictory or downright illegible.

*Robert M. Bleiberg*

Sometimes you can observe a lot just watching.

*Yogi Berra*

Criticism comes when you do something. Do nothing and escape criticism.

*Mac Brunson*

There's just no way we can always make the right decision. That doesn't mean you're an idiot. But it does focus on how serious the consequences could be if you turn out to be wrong.

*Peter Bernstein*

You are a poor specimen if you can't stand the pressure of adversity.

*Proverbs 24: 10*

Some rich people are poor and some poor people are rich.

*Proverbs 13:7*

The Lord hates cheating and delights in honesty.

*Proverbs 11:1*

Sins can be forgiven. Stupidity lasts forever.

*Norman Brinker*

You get what you tolerate.

*Jack Evans*

It is that the influence of a really good person lives on in the benefits he confers upon others, and that influence never really fades. Courage and integrity are among the most valuable virtues of humanity outlasting even death itself.

*Dr. Ashley Montague*

Ill-gotten gain brings no lasting happiness; right living does.

*Proverbs 10:2*

No matter where you place the weak player—the baseball will always find him.

*Jimmy Roe*

Ain't nuthin in life is dead solid perfect.

*Dan Jenkins*

Whatever happens, the sun will rise in the east and go down in the west.

*Roger Lipton*

My son, how I will rejoice if you become a man of common sense.

*Proverbs 23: 15*

The riskiest moment is where you are right. That's when you're in the most trouble, because you tend to overstay the good decisions.

*Peter Bernstein*

If an offer seems too good to be true, you can rest assured that it is.

*Dick Davis*

The snake you see is not the one that bites you.

*Al Goldman*

"No one can take anything away from you that you are not willing to give up.

*Don Haskins*

Wisdom is not a product of schooling but of the lifelong attempt to acquire it.

*Albert Einstein*

Get the facts at any price and hold on tightly to all the good sense you can get.

*Proverbs 23:23*

You have to reinvent yourself all of the time.

*Robert Pritikin*

It's a capital mistake to theorize before one has data. Insensibly, one begins to twist facts to suit theories instead of theories to suit facts.

*Sherlock Holmes*

In other words, without good information, you won't see things as they really are—you'll see them as you think they are.

*Anonymous*

You can't second guess yourself. When it's over with...it's over with. So don't worry about it.

*Tom Landry*

**Horse Sense. Street Smarts.**

When's the best time to stop talking? Probably now. A story is told about FDR when he was a young lawyer. He heard his opponent summarize a case before the jury in eloquent, emotional, but lengthy appeal. Sensing the jury was restless, FDR is reported to have said, You have heard the evidence. You have also listened to a brilliant orator. If you believe him, and disbelieve the evidence, you will decide in his favor. That's all I have to say. He won. Overstate and bore. Understate and score. When a baseball umpire says, "Strike three!" He doesn't have to add "Yer out." That's what strike three means.

*Anonymous*

Changing your mind is saying you have a better idea.

*Les Wexner*

Give a man a fish and you feed him for a day. Teach a man to fish and you feed him for a lifetime.

*Lao Tzu*

If you inject humor into what you say, people will listen to you just to hear what you're going to say.

*Lou Holtz*

Ideas reach their greatest popularity and broadest distribution when they become irrelevant, obsolete, or downright dangerous.

*Scott Burns*

The five cardinal sins of Rome—and of all past great nations are described in Edward Gibbon's The Decline and Fall of the Roman Empire. These five reasons are as follows:

1. The increase of divorce and breakdown of the family.

2. The spiral rise of taxes and extravagant spending.

3. The mounting craze for pleasure and brutality in sports.

4. The building of gigantic armaments while failing to realize that the real enemy was the moral decay within.

5. The decay of religion into a mere form, leaving the people without any guide.

*Edward Gibbon*

He who truly knows has no reason to shout.

*Leonardo da Vinci*

At the end of the day, all you have left is a good name.

*Jim Morris' grandfather*

When you can, you want to plan for tomorrow, but don't worry about it so that you don't enjoy today.

*Lou Holtz*

There cannot be mental atrophy in any person who continues to observe, to remember what he observes and to seek answers for his unceasing hows and whys about things.

*Alexander Graham Bell*

Many things can happen to a promise:

A promise can be broken.

It can be ignored, or simply forgotten.

A promise can be put on the back burner.

It can be attributed to someone else,

Or just lost in the shuffle.

A promise can become procrastination.

It can become puffery,

Or just wishful thinking.

Of course, there is one more thing that can happen to a promise.

A promise can be kept.

*Financial Times*

Know what's right, avoid what's wrong.

*Lou Holtz*

No matter what you do in life, when you give your word, you keep it.

*Max Weitzenhoffer*

Most of my advances were by mistake. You uncover what is when you get rid of what isn't. How often I found where I should be going only by setting out for somewhere else.

*Buckminster Fuller*

Freedom is not the natural state of mankind. It is a rare and wonderful achievement. It will take an understanding of what freedom is, of where the dangers to freedom come from. It will take the courage to act on that understanding if we are not only to preserve the freedoms that we have, but to realize the full potential of a truly free society.

*Milton Friedman*

I don't know the key to success, but the key to failure is trying to please everybody.

*Bill Cosby*

The art of teaching is also to know when to stop.

*B.K.S. Iyengar*

The more we know of our own failings, the easier it becomes to understand other people and why they act as they do.

*Bernard Baruch*

If you don't know where you are going, you might wind up someplace else.

*Yogi Berra*

The future is hard to predict because no one knows what is going to happen.

*Vladimir Rockov*

Vision without execution is hallucination.

*Albert Einstein*

An appeaser is one who feeds a crocodile, hoping it will eat him last.

*Winston Churchill*

If a man can only have one kind of sense, let him have common sense. If he has that and uncommon sense, too, he is not too far from genius.

*Henry Ward Beecher*

I think it's important that you prepare for lean times in good times.

*Sandy Weill*

Trust instinct to the end, even though you can give no reason.

*Ralph Waldo Emerson*

Pictures are for entertainment. Messages should be sent by Western Union.

*Samuel Goldwyn*

Intuition is a highly complex form of reasoning that is based on years of experience and learning and on facts, patterns, concepts, procedures and abstractions stored in one's head.

*Kurt Matzler, Johannes Kepler ,& Todd A. Mooradian*

Whatever the mind of man can conceive and believe, it can achieve.

*Napoleon Hill*

You need to listen to what wakes you up in the middle of the night. I've learned that if something keeps you up at night, don't discount it. Make sure and listen.

*Paul Orfalea*

It is better to be rich and healthy than sick and poor.

*Anonymous*

If the whole body were an eye, where would the sense of hearing be? If the whole body were an ear, where would the sense of smell be?

But in fact God has placed the parts in the body, every one of them, just as he wanted them to be.

If they were all one part, where would the body be?

*1 Corinthians 12:17-19*

Every failure carries within itself the seed of an equivalent advantage.

*Andrew Carnegie*

The wish is the father of the thought and the thought is the father of the result.

*Dick Perkins*

Intuition is given only to him who has undergone long preparation to receive it.

*Louis Pasteur*

Gaining additional experience is the first step toward improving intuition.

*Kurt Matzler, Johannes Kepler, & Todd A. Mooradian*

A liar is a coward afraid to tell the truth.

*Father John Walsh*

Forgive those who least deserve it.

*Bill Curry*

There is no calamity greater than lavish desires.

*Chinese Philosopher*

Never underestimate the power of no.

*Ray Charles*

I cannot trust a man to control others who cannot control himself.

*Robert E. Lee*

Surround yourself with people who aggravate you.

*Paul Orfalea's father*

I have yet to find the man, however exalted his station, who did not do better work and put forth greater effort under a spirit of approval than under a spirit of criticism.

*Charles M. Schwab*

In boom times, people get complacent, especially if they haven't been through a bust cycle.

*Joe Morgan*

Talent, to me, is wanting something badly enough to work for it.

*Tim Cox*

Find something you love to do and you'll never have to work a day in your life.

*Harvey MacKay*

We become what we think about.

*Earl Nightingale*

You can't copy somebody, because when you do and a new situation arises, you find yourself wondering what the person you're trying to copy would do instead of what you should do.

*Don Drysdale*

There is a difference between involvement and commitment. In a ham and egg breakfast, the chicken is involved; the pig is committed.

*Anonymous*

It never hurts to ask.

*Ray Charles*

Be confident that whatever you can actually succeed in doing is going to be enough to satisfy you. If you want to play like Vladimir Horowitz, you are going to be disappointed. You have to be confident that whatever you end up performing, it will be satisfying.

*William F. Buckley*

The more education you have, the more choices you have.

*Ike Vanden Eykel*

Be yourself and do what you love. You never know what you're capable of.

*David Novak*

When the cup is full, carry it carefully.

*Andy McCarthy*

One cool judgment is worth a thousand hasty counsels. The thing to be supplied is light not heat.

*Woodrow Wilson*

Don't get down too much when you're going through bad times, but don't get too exuberant when you're going through good times, because neither of those are representative of the long term.

*David O'Reilly*

Nothing is as destabilizing as stability. Profit-seeking people will take more financial risk when they believe the coast is clear. By taking bigger chances, they unwittingly make the world unsafe all over again.

*Anonymous*

The future is not going to be like yesterday, it's not going to be like today, and it sure as heck won't be what you think it's going to be.

*James F. Chambers, Jr.*

You don't have to be completely stupid to feed cattle, but it helps.

*Wayne Cleveland*

The hangover is directly proportional to the binge.

*Warren Buffett*

What everybody knows isn't worth knowing.

*Anonymous*

I find it best to be on the side of the minority since it is always the most intelligent.

*Goethe*

Show me a good loser and I'll show you a loser.

*Red Auerbach*

Where all think alike, no one thinks very much. If two people agree with you, the chances are you are wrong.

*Walter Lippman*

One of the responses to crisis is entrepreneurship. It's sort of like a forest fire. The ashes of the catastrophe are the fertilizer of the next growth.

*David Birch*

I borrow only what I feel I can comfortably pay back.

*Harold Simmons*

You can't beat the tranquility of the outdoors.

*Bobby Knight*

Sometimes you can observe a lot just watching.

*Yogi Berra*

The biggest risk in life is not risking.

*Dr. Robert Anthony*

Discovery consists of seeing what everybody has seen and thinking what nobody has thought.

*Albert Szent-Gyorgyi*

Courage is grace under pressure.

*Ernest Hemingway*

The supreme test of generalship is to know when to retreat and have the courage to do it.

*The Duke of Wellington*

Selling and saving capital is living to invest again another day.

*Don Hodges*

Bring me men to match my mountains. Bring me men with empires in their purpose and new eras in their brains.

*Sam Walter Foss*

"The public's perception of what is good lingers long past the time the reality ends.

*Anonymous*

Never mistake motion for action.

*Ernest Hemingway*

I'm more concerned about the return of my investment than return on my investment.

*Will Rogers*

The bad part is that good jobs don't need coaches. The bad jobs take a long time to turn around.

*Bum Phillips*

Do the best you can with what you've got.

*Ed Kelly*

Plans get you into things, but you got to work your way out.

*Will Rogers*

Truth is the first casualty of politics.

*Dee Miller*

Nothing in life brings more happiness than serving a cause greater than yourself.

*John McCain*

Idleness and pride tax with a heavier hand than kings and parliaments.

*Benjamin Franklin*

Leave all the afternoon for exercise and recreation, which are as necessary as reading. I will rather say more necessary because health is worth more than learning.

*Thomas Jefferson*

If people aren't better off with what you are doing for them, find something else to do.

*Wes Hickman*

A name is made up of little promises kept to the letter. It is made up of faithfulness, loyalty, honesty, of efficiency in your work. In short, a name is the blueprint of the thing we call character. You ask, 'What's in a name?' I answer, 'Just about everything you do.'

*The Jewish Press*

A corporation's a fictitious person with no conscience, no character, no integrity.

*Dee Miller*

Do that which is right in the sight of all, knowing that nothing is hidden from God; and God, who sees the invisible, will reward you.

*Matthew 6:4*

Never look backwards or you'll fall down the stairs.

*Rudyard Kipling*

What the wise man does at the beginning, the fool does at the end.

*Warren Buffet*

I assume that the future will be much like the past, but sometimes it isn't.

*Ben Stein*

Wealth can be acquired in many ways, and precious metals and gems can be purchased, but even the most exclusive retail store cannot sell you a good reputation. It is not a commodity to be purchased or bartered; it can only be obtained through a life devoted to upholding high ideals and personal values—even when it's not convenient or expedient.

*Robert J. Tamasy*

I will, to the best of my experience and ability, do what it takes to minimize the damage and recover. My orientation will be, the past is gone; today and the future require my attention.

*Al Frank*

Reputation is what others think of you, but character is who you are in the dark.

*Anonymous*

Those who have knowledge don't predict. Those who predict don't have knowledge.

*Lao Tzu*

Be understanding to your perceived enemies.

Be loyal to your friends.

Be strong enough to face the world each day.

Be weak enough to know you cannot do everything alone.

Be generous to those who need your help.

Be frugal with what you need yourself.

Be wise enough to know that you do not know everything.

Be foolish enough to believe in miracles.

Be willing to share your joys.

Be willing to share the sorrows of others.

Be a leader when you see a path others have missed.

Be a follower when you are shrouded by the mists of uncertainty.

Be first to congratulate an opponent who succeeds.

Be last to criticize a colleague who fails.

Be sure where your next step will fall, so that you will not tumble.

Be sure of your final destination, in case you are going the wrong way.

Be loving to those who love you.

Be loving to those who do not love you; they may change.

Above all, be yourself.

Just Be Yourself!

*Anonymous*


There is no education like adversity.

*Benjamin Disraeli*


If you are not telling me what you believe, then you're not doing either me a service or yourself a service, or, ultimately, the organization you're serving.

*Gen. George Marshall*


The key to everything is patience. You get the chicken by hatching the egg, not by smashing it.

*Arnold Glasgow*


There are three reasons we can't do it: the first one is we don't have the money, and it doesn't make a difference about the other two.

*Tom Pickens*


That, which doesn't kill you, makes you stronger.

*George Roberts*


**Horse Sense. Street Smarts.**

I think failure, by definition, gets a bad rap. The assumption that it is an irretrievable error is simply not true.

*Ann Richards*

How do you avoid mistakes? Improve your judgment. How do you improve your judgment? By making mistakes.

*Anonymous*

From each according to his ability; to each according to his need.

*Karl Marx*

My grace is sufficient for you, for my power is made perfect in weakness.

*2 Corinthians 12:9*

If you have to cheat to win, there is no pride in winning.

*Otto Mangold*

A liar is a coward; he is afraid to tell the truth.

*Father John Walsh*

The receiver of a gift is happy. The giver is blessed.

*John Wilkinson*

There is no substitute for knowledge. To this day, I read three newspapers a day. It is impossible to read a paper without being exposed to ideas. And ideas...more than money...are the real currency for success.

*Eli Broad*

Honest mistakes are like skinned knees—very painful but they heal quickly.

*Ross Perot*

Failures that transform a businessman into a supercautious individual can cripple.

*Trammell Crow*

There is no class so pitiably wretched as that which possesses money and nothing else.

*Andrew Carnegie*

I will amputate a limb to save a life...a part can't control the whole to the destruction of the whole.

*Abraham Lincoln*

Nothing good happens after midnight.

*Alma Hodges*

God will never deal you more than you can, with His help, handle.

*Alma Hodges*

The two most powerful warriors are patience and time.

*Leo Tolstoy*

Have more than thou showest. Speak less than thou knowest. Lend less than thou owest.

*King Lear's Fool*

The art of being wise is the art of knowing what to overlook.

*William James*

If government spending were the path to prosperity, then the Soviet Union would have won the Cold War.

*Steve Forbes*

To thine own self be true.

*William Shakespeare*

Smooth seas do not make skillful sailors.

*African proverb*

To thine own self be true. It's not just you can be anything you want to be, but be clear about who you really are and trust in that. You don't need to be or do anything to please somebody else, but to really follow your own heart's desire and be really true to yourself. It is very much about being at peace with that and let that be your guidepost.

*Beth Ann Kaminkow*

Facts are stubborn things, and whatever may be our wishes, our inclinations, or the dictates of our passions, they cannot alter the state of facts and evidence.

*John Adams*

I don't want my players getting on the officials ever, no matter what the situation. If sports are to have educational benefits, you have to learn to handle the bad calls of the world and get on with your business.

*Pete Newell*

Whatever is true, whatever is noble, whatever is right, whatever is pure, whatever is lovely, whatever is admirable, if anything is excellent or praiseworthy—think about such things.

*Philippians 4:8*

The great economic era we are entering will give splendid opportunity to the young men of the future. One often hears the men of this new generation say that they do not have the chances that their fathers and grandfathers had. How little they know of the disadvantages from which we suffered.

*John D. Rockefeller, Sr.*

Everyone is a hero in his own movie.

*Max Batzer*

Every family is a soap opera; all you need is a script writer.

*Ed Rice*

Grasp the subject, words will follow.

*Cato the Elder*

Your children are never too old for you to tell them that you love them.

*Fred W. Frailey*

To be persuasive we must be believable; to be believable we must be credible; to be credible we must be truthful.

*Edward R. Murrow*

Yesterday is a cancelled check. Tomorrow is a promissory note. Today is the only cash you have, so spend it wisely.

*Kay Lyons*

Judge a man by his questions rather than by his answers.

*Voltaire*

When you die the only thing you're going to die with is the reputation you've created as a person. You're going to be remembered for the type of person you were and the character you had.

*Pop Rosenberg*

Life is the sum of all your choices.

*Albert Camus*

Just because something doesn't do what you planned it to do, doesn't mean it's useless.

*Thomas Edison*

Don't let your ego get too close to your position, so that if your position gets shot down, your ego doesn't go with it.

*Colin Powell*

You've got to go out on a limb sometimes because that is where the fruit is.

*Will Rogers*

When we die, the only thing we can take with us is love.

*Patrick Swayze*

**Horse Sense. Street Smarts.**

You don't sell to people: you get people to buy from you. You say to yourself, 'If I were in their position, why would I buy this product I have to sell?'

*Bill Rosenberg*

Intense concentration hour after hour can bring out resources in people they didn't know they had.

*Edwin Land*

He who wishes to rule others must learn to rule himself...must undertake tasks not because they are pleasant or interesting but because they contribute in some small but necessary way to the proper and wise exercise of power.

*Goethe*

What we eat, how we respond to stress, whether or not we smoke cigarettes, how much exercise we get, the quality of our relationships, and the social support can be as powerful as drugs and surgery.

*Deepak Chopra, Dean Ornish, Rustum Roy, & Andrew Weil*

High achievement always takes place in the framework of high expectation.

*Charles Kettering*

The most rewarding things you do in life are often the ones that look like they cannot be done.

*Arnold Palmer*

Before you lead, you have to know where you're going. Before you lead, you have to be ready to serve. Before you lead, you have to default to responsibility.

*Donovan Campbell*

I feel it's wrong to dwell on the negative side. Usually there's a positive and, in the end, I think, one gets further trying to be balanced in one's point of view.

*David Rockefeller*

Somebody has to do something and it's just incredibly pathetic that it has to be us.

*Jerry Garcia*

When you got nothing, you got nothing to lose.

*Bob Dylan*

He has not learned the lesson of life who does not every day surmount a fear.

*Ralph Waldo Emerson*

Create a balance between home and work because troubles on either front bleed into the other.

*Bob Seelert*

Stay calm, cool and don't overreact to criticism or stress.

*Bob Seelert*

Tell me who you're with and I'll tell you who you are.

*Spanish proverb*

Don't waste time in bad situations. Don't waste time in a bad relationship or six months on a job you don't like. You've gotta live life today.

*Eric Castillo-Wilson*

The key to surviving change is to be able to turn on a dime. You have to embrace new ideas even when you don't like them. You don't have time to dwell on the past and you have to prove yourself every day. Get up early, work hard and be grateful. Be brief and direct. Always ask for feedback and don't cry when you get it.

*Elaine Agather*

Make peace with your past so it won't screw up the present.

*Regina Brett*

Tongue double brings trouble.

*Poor Richard*

You don't control your fate, but you do control the formation of your character.

*Rod Dreher*

You can't live a perfect day without doing something for someone who will never be able to repay you.

*John Wooden*

A government that is big enough to give you everything you want is big enough to take away everything you have.

*Gerald Ford*

All that needs to happen for evil to win is for good people to stand by and do nothing.

*Edwin Meese III*

You don't retire! People who are in jobs they don't like retire.

*Bea Arthur*

Behind America's balancing act lies a common set of civic virtues that celebrate hard work, thrift, integrity, selfreliance, and modesty—virtues that grew out of the pervasiveness of religion.

*Alexis de Tocqueville*

The secret to happiness is to do what you love to do with people you love.

*From the movie Night at the Museum*

Your choice of people to associate with both personally and business-wise is one of the most important choices you make.

*Brian Tracy*

The true idealist preaches not class hatred but universal love; not to redistribute the wealth but multiply the wealth; not more regulation but more freedom; not security but opportunity. The true idealist is the missionary for individual freedom and competition.

*Sir John Templeton*

I believe in the dynamic creativity of capitalism and its self correcting, if you just allow it to self-correct.

*John Mackey*

A gossip tells everything, but a true friend will keep a secret.

*Proverbs 11:13*

There is always a well known solution to every human problem—neat, plausible, and wrong. Error flows down the channel of history like some great stream of lava or infinitely lethargic glacier.

*H.L. Mencken*

What you gain by doing evil won't help you at all.

*Proverbs 10:2*

It's stupid and embarrassing to give an answer before you listen.

*Proverbs 18:131*

Wisdom is worth more than silver; it makes you much richer than gold. Wisdom is more valuable than precious jewels; nothing you want compares with her.

*Proverbs 3:14-15*

You will say the wrong thing if you talk too much—so be sensible and watch what you say.

*Proverbs 10:19*

Hiding hateful thoughts behind smooth talk is like coating a clay pot with a cheap glaze.

*Proverbs 26:23*

A kind answer soothes angry feelings, but harsh words stir them up.

*Proverbs 15:1*

It's better to be honest and poor than to be dishonest and rich.

*Proverbs 16*

A friend is always a friend, and relatives are born to share our troubles.

*Proverbs 17:17*

Caring for the poor is lending to the LORD, and you will be well repaid.

*Proverbs 19:17*

If you stop learning, you will forget what you already know.

*Proverbs 19:27*

Metacognition—thinking about thinking. Pilots have a different name for it. They call it deliberate calm because staying calm under fraught circumstances requires both conscious effort and regular practice. Pilots aren't the only people who are forced to act in crisis. No matter how difficult or unprecedented the problem, we have the ability to look past our primal emotions and carefully think about how we need to think. Metacognition allows a person to remain calm when every bone in his body is telling him to panic.

*Jonah Lehrer*

It's smart to be patient, but it's stupid to lose your temper.

*Proverbs 14:29*

No matter how humble your beginnings, you have to trust in your dreams and never forget your roots.

*Joe Raposo*

There is a very thin line between survival and success. Staying on the right side of that line is critical and cash is king.

*Richard Branson*

Sacrifices must be made.

*Otto Lilienthal*

**Realism**

Believe what you see, not what you hear, and not what you read, as what you hear and what you read may be opinions.

*Richard Perkins*

A good reputation at the time of death is better than loving care at the time of birth.

*Ecclesiastes 7:1*

When a good person gives in to the wicked, it's like dumping garbage in a stream of clear water.

*Proverbs 25:26*

Giving an honest answer is a sign of true friendship.

*Proverbs 24:26*

Even if good people fall seven times, they will get back up.

*Proverbs 24:26*

Don't be a heavy drinker or stuff yourself with food.

*Proverbs 23:20*

Battles are won by listening to advice and making a lot of plans.

*Proverbs 24:26*

Losing self-control leaves you as helpless as a city without a wall.

*Proverbs 25:28*

It's better to take hold of a mad dog by the ears than to take part in someone else's argument.

*Proverbs 26:17*

Broken promises are worse than rain clouds that don't bring rain.

*Proverbs 25:14*

Losing your temper causes a lot of trouble, but staying calm settles arguments.

*Proverbs 15:18*

Everything on earth has its own time and its own season. There is a time for birth and death, planting and reaping, for killing and healing, destroying and building, for crying and laughing, weeping and dancing, for throwing stones and gathering stones, embracing and parting. There is a time for finding and losing, keeping and giving, for tearing and sewing, listening and speaking. There is also a time for love and hate, for war and peace.

*Ecclesiastes 3: 1-8*

Treat people as you would like to be treated, but don't let anyone mistake kindness for weakness.

*Art Rooney*

When you and someone else can't get along, don't gossip about it.

*Proverbs 25:9*

It's better to be poor and live right, than to be rich and dishonest.

*Proverbs 28:6*

I talk a lot about the pain of discipline or the pain of regret. You really only have two choices in life. I'd rather have the pain of discipline than feel regret.

*Joseph J. Plumeri*

I have to fight every single day to live my true life. I don't ever want to come home saying, 'I should have spoken my mind.'

*Sandra Bullock*

To err is human. To cover up, is plain dumb.

*Gretchen Morgenson*

A lot of people feel as you grow older you become a center of wisdom. I do not subscribe to such a theory. What really happens is you make your share of mistakes and, I suppose, the more successful people learn by these errors. Perhaps you could sum this idea up in a word: experience.

*Art Rooney*

**Realism**

The hunger for status can be, and often is, as profound as hunger for food.

*Lionel Tiger*

Leadership is the lifting of a man's vision to higher sights, the raising of a man's performance to a higher standard, the building of a man's personality beyond its normal limitations.

*Peter Drucker*

Who is always in trouble? Who argues and fights? Who has cuts and bruises? Whose eyes are red? Everyone who stays up late, having just one more drink. Don't even look at that colorful stuff bubbling up in the glass! It goes down so easily, but later it bites like a poisonous snake. You will see weird things! And your mind will play tricks on you. You will feel tossed about like someone trying to sleep on a ship in a storm. You will be bruised all over, without even remembering how it all happened. And you will lie awake asking, When will morning come, so I can drink some more?

*Proverbs 23:29-35*

All compromise is based on give and take, but, there can be no give and take on fundamentals.

*Mohandas Ghandi*

Your mind is like a compulsive yes-man who echoes whatever you want to believe. Psychologists call this mental gremlin 'confirmation bias.' A recent analysis of psychological studies with nearly 8000 participants concluded that people are twice as likely to seek information that confirms what they already believe as they are to consider evidence that would challenge those beliefs.

*Jason Zweig*

If you have an IQ of 150 and you want to be an investment manager, sell 30 points. You don't need the other 30. Emotional stability and peace are much more important than having an IQ of 150.

*Charlie Munger*

The true measure of a man is how he treats someone who can do him absolutely no good.

*Anonymous*

Followers may forgive a man for a great deal: incompetence, ignorance, insecurity, or bad manners; but they will not forgive him a lack of integrity.

*Peter Drucker*

Don't drink. Don't smoke. Don't retire.

*Ebby Halliday*

Sin will always take you further than you wanted to go, keep you longer than you wanted to stay, and cost you more than you wanted to pay.

*Dr. James C. Denison*

Soldiers admire leaders who are focused and don't overreact.

*Lt. Gen. Robert Cone*

Don't borrow problems.

*Alma Hodges*

If the horse is fed enough oats, some will pass through to the sparrows.

*John Kenneth Galbraith*

When you're talking to someone, look them in the eye. Always tell the truth.

*Bobbi Brown*

Sell the stock when stories about the CEO move from the financial pages to the social pages.

*Ed Rice*

I don't care who you are and what you do, you have to start at the bottom.

*Bobbi Brown*

When you play football, you learn to take success, you learn to take defeat, you learn to live with it and you learn from your bad experiences, and you go on and try to improve yourself. You never quit and you have a positive attitude.

*George Blanda*

Openly apologizing has the potential to turn a problem into a teachable moment for employees, thereby preventing a repeat occurrence.

*Paul Levy*

America's finest historical hours have not come when we were sitting on top of a massive bull market. Our finest hour has come from when we were hungry and worried, and instead of grumbling about it, started to put our shoulder to the wheel

*Don Hays*

If you choose to work, you will succeed; if you don't, you will fail. If you neglect your work, you will dislike it; if you do it well, you will enjoy it. If you join little cliques, you will be selfsatisfied; if you make friends widely, you will be interesting. If you gossip, you will be slandered; if you mind your own business, you will be liked. If you act like a boor, you will be despised; if you act like a human being, you will be respected.

If you spurn wisdom, wise people will spurn you; if you seek wisdom, they will seek you. If you adopt a pose of boredom, you will be a bore; if you show vitality, you will be alive. If you spend your free time playing bridge, you will be a good bridge player; if you spend it reading, discussing and thinking of things that matter, you will be an educated person.

*Sidney Earle Smith*

I guess, underlying it all, I believe in capitalism, I believe in the American spirit to get down in the trenches and turn things around when they get bad. Companies go through cycles just like sports teams do, and you have to watch those cycles and try to invest in them at the proper time. But I really believe in equity investment and in the long-term outlook for America.

There will always be new companies, new trends, new inventions—and I might add that those new blades of grass will come from individuals and not from the government. I look forward to the future and think we've got a great future with profitable investment opportunities ahead of us. But there are times we have to be cautious and careful.

*Don Hodges*

Never make a promise you cannot keep and say nothing rather than something if you are in doubt.

*Joe Wilson, Sr.*

The best time to plant a tree was twenty years ago. In the event you didn't plant one then, the second best time is now.

*Boone Pickens*

It's okay to feel conflicting emotions of anger, anxiety, fear, hopelessness, etc. Just keep them balanced.

*Terry Wise*

Talking about your problems won't change them; it will help you deal with them.

*Terry Wise*

Only God knows the end of the beginning.

*John Hagee*

A company that openly apologizes does more than merely take public responsibility for its actions—it also signals to its own employees that certain practices are unacceptable.

*Natasha Singer*

We never lie. You don't lie to your own doctor, you don't lie to your own attorney, and you don't lie to your employees. And if you never lie, then when it hits the fan and somebody says you're wrong—you can say 'No, I'm not' and they'll believe you.

*Gordon M. Bethune*

If we do not use our freedom to defend our freedom, we will lose our freedom.

*John Hagee*

If you want to know how long 90 days is, just borrow a 90 day loan from the bank.

*Anonymous*

When people are humiliated or embarrassed, they don't forget the person who did it.

*Ralph Reiger*

I think you have to compare yourself with the best to learn.

*Clyde Aspevig*

Don't think that I imagine I'll become a great artist. It's simply that I want to do that to which I am drawn,

*Peter Tchaikovsky*

The only thing we have to fear is fear itself,

*Franklin Roosevelt*

If you're not in control of your calendar, you're not in control

*Don Regan*

People remember acts of kindness for a lifetime.

*Terry Wise*

The last temptation is the greatest treason: to do the right deed for the wrong reason.

*T.S. Eliot*

If your wife cooks dinner for you, make certain you get home on time.

*Raymond Hollingsworth*

Fame is toxic. It destroys a lot of people.

*David Kupelian*

If you have any talent, it is God's gift to you. If you use that talent, it is your gift to God.

*Red Skelton*

Think ahead.

*Freddie Hodges*

It's all about doing the work. It's a dream until you write it down, and then it's a goal.

*Emmitt Smith, III*

True wealth is really measured in lives you touch, not dollars you have.

*Dan Duncan*

If China does well or Russia, it won't make America any less prosperous.

*Warren Buffett*

Tell it like it is, and if you tell it like it is, you don't get egg on your face.

*Charles E. Grassley*

Everything that has happened in my life...that I thought was a crushing event at the time, has turned out for the better.

*Warren Buffett*

Thoughts become things.

*Colt McCoy*

Prepare for open and closed doors.

*Brad McCoy*

Success is getting what you want and happiness is wanting what you get.

*Warren Buffett*

Science cannot produce the 'meaning of life' nor can it tell us the right moral values.

*Richard P. Feynman*

I think the words 'I don't know' is a little phrase much avoided and I don't really know why. I just turned 50 and there's still plenty I don't know, and that's something that I often tell my staff. If you don't know something, it's just so much better to say so.

*Rachel Ashwell*

Ask nothing that is not clearly right and submit to nothing that is wrong.

*Andrew Jackson*

If the facts available justify a decision at the time, it will also be correct in the future.

*Harry Truman*

Bitterness is a terrible temptation to harbour your own troubles and problems and indulge in self-pity. Bitterness very often leads to depression.

*Elisabeth Elliott*

Failure is the best teacher.

*Harry Markopolos*

You will be remembered in life by the problems you solve or the problems you create.

*John Hagee*

Let your light shine before men in such a way that they may see your good works and glorify your Father who is in heaven.

*Matthew 5:16*

If you have unconditional love, it doesn't matter if you win.

*George W. Bush*

Opening wide the window of transparency not only builds knowledge, it creates trust.

*Vineet Nayar*

Sacrifices must be made.

*Otto Lilienthal*

I'd rather be wrong with the cash than wrong with the horse.

*Wayne Cleveland (on the possibility of buying a much desired horse)*

If you begin with a prayer, you can think more clearly and make fewer mistakes.

*Sir John Templeton*

I am convinced that a great deal of depression is the fruit of bitterness, which is unresolved sin or anger or pain.

*Elisabeth Elliott*

Texas is a state of mind.

*John Steinbeck*

Landscape painting: food for the soul

*Robert Pummill*

Never follow the crowd.

*Bernard Baruch*

A climate of fear is our best friend.

*Warren Buffett*

**Realism**

Choose the harder right instead of the easier wrong.

*Bob McDonald*

The whole point of America is that we all live better than we did anywhere else; the Blacks, the Asians, the Irish, the Germans...it's better for all of us here than anywhere else.

*Ben Stein's father*

It's the lows that make us who we are.

*Marie Osmond*

Today, people can see into your life farther, faster, and cheaper than ever before. You are on candid camera, so be good.

*Tom Friedman*

You have brains in your head. You have feet in your shoes. You can steer yourself in any direction you choose. You're on your own and you know what you know. You are the guy who'll decide where to go.

*Dr. Seuss*

Trust but verify.

*Ronald Reagan*

We need encouragement a lot more than we admit, even to ourselves.

*Orson Welles*

Ultimately, the only way to enjoy a good reputation is to earn it by living with integrity.

*Dov Seidman*

When it's raining gold, reach for a bucket, not a thimble.

*Warren Buffett*

Wherever attention flows, money will follow.

*Kevin Kelly*

One of the things I learned in the military is how you can accomplish more as a team than you can as an individual.

*Bob McDonald*

The biggest single waste of time in earth is wishing things were different.

*Don Connelly*

There's no right way to do the wrong thing.

*Waylon Jennings*

Judges are lawyers in robes.

*John Stossel*

Freedom in economic arrangements is itself a component of freedom broadly understood, so economic freedom is an end in itself. Economic freedom is also an indispensable means toward the achievement of political freedom.

*Milton Friedman*

Society cannot exist, unless a controlling power upon will and appetite be placed somewhere; and the less of it there is within, the more there must be without.

*Sir Edmund Burke*

The only thing necessary for evil to triumph is for good men to do nothing.

*Sir Edmund Burke*

The only way to get the best of an argument is to avoid it.

*Dale Carnegie*

The Lord searches every heart and understands every motive behind the thoughts.

*1 Chronicles 28:9*

Always do what is best for the client.

*Ray Dusek*

The first thing is character...before money or anything else. Money cannot buy it.

*J. Pierpont Morgan*

Don't be afraid of the phrase, 'I don't know.' If you don't know the answer, don't try to bluff. If you're at fault, take the blame. If you're wrong, apologize. A wise person once said, 'If you always tell the truth, you never have to remember anything.'

*The Manager's Intelligence Report*

Years may wrinkle the skin, but to give up interest wrinkles the soul. You are as young as your faith, as old as your doubt; as young as your self-confidence, as old as your fear; as young as your hope, as old as your despair.

In the central place of every heart there is a recording chamber. So long as it receives messages of beauty, hope, cheer and courage, so long are you young. When your heart is covered with the snows of pessimism and the ice of cynicism, then, and then only, are you grown old. And then, indeed as the ballad says, you just fade away.

*Gen. Douglas MacArthur*

You learn about people by listening. I mean really listening. People eventually reveal themselves when they talk.

*Gayle Earls*

Play fair. Put things back where you found them. Clean up your own mess. Live a balanced life – learn some and think some and draw and paint and sing and dance and play and work every day some.

*Robert L. Fulgham*

I present, reiterate, and glorify the obvious, because the obvious is what people want.

*Dale Carnegie*

**Horse Sense. Street Smarts.**

I hope we have once again reminded the people that man is not free unless government is limited. There's a clear cause and effect here that is as neat and predictable as a law of physics: as government expands, liberty contracts.

*Ronald Reagan*

Never tolerate injustice or corruption. Always be drastically independent. Never be afraid to attack wrong.

*Joseph Pulitzer*

I believe the public has a sixth sense for detecting insincerity, and we run a tremendous risk if we try to make other people believe in something we don't believe in. Somehow our sin will find us out.

*Bruce Barton*

Do not be afraid of mistakes, providing you do not make the same one twice.

*Eleanor Roosevelt*

Honesty is the cornerstone of all success, without which confidence and ability to perform shall cease to exist.

*Mary Kay Ash*

A person who says 'maybe' essentially puts recipient B on hold. Some 'maybe' people are trying to stall, buy time, work up their nerve to decline the offer or see if a better one comes along. Parents use 'maybe' to soften a negative to a child. Ditto bosses and their employees.

*Prudence Gourguechon*

I don't know how many of your problems that you've kicked down the road ended up getting better later on, but in my life, it's almost none of them.

*Kyle Bass*

Everyone has to do something wrong.

*Clark Hodges*

Most people aspire to do better and most people actually want their kids to do better than themselves.

*Tony Blair*

If a magician reveals some of his tricks, the audience can entertain themselves for awhile, but if he reveals all his tricks, they won't pay to see the show.

*Stacey Haefele*

You have to recognize that the values that kids have are the crucial things that will make or break them.

*Thomas Sowell*

The judge's job is not to have empathy; his job is to carry out the law as written. And if it is a bad law, it is up to the legislature to change it.

*Thomas Sowell*

We can have all the knowledge in the world, but it is wisdom we need to have.

*Marie Osmond*

Stay in the middle of the road. Don't go to the extreme right of the road nor the extreme left.

*Cybil Shepherd's grandmother*

Everybody has a plan until they get punched in the mouth.

*Mike Tyson*

Life isn't about whether your glass is half-full or half-empty. It's about drinking from the glass.

*Scott Burns*

Never invest in any idea you cannot illustrate with a crayon.

*Peter Lynch*

**Horse Sense. Street Smarts.**

I predict future happiness for Americans if they can prevent the government from wasting the labors of the people under the pretense of taking care of them.

*Thomas Jefferson*

My reading of history convinces me that most bad government results from too much government.

*Thomas Jefferson*

Both bankers and borrowers are at risk if trust erodes. Trust is critical to successful business. Studies have shown that if one party cheats on one end, the other party feels more entitled to cheat. It's not the most noble way, but it's human nature, and it becomes a race to the bottom.

*Tom Donaldson*

The erosion of the ethics of keeping promises will be a cancer for society.

*E. Phillip Davis*

The long run is a misleading guide to current affairs. In the long run, we are all dead.

*John Maynard Keynes*

When you're out of town as much as I am, you're subject to a lot of temptations. There was always a bar and some good looking gals inside, and it wasn't hard to get some action if you wanted. I am as weak as the next guy, and so I decided to limit my exposure. I still practice that and encourage my people to head for the house when you get through.

*Boone Pickens*

If people and relationships are the sine qua non of enterprise success, and I flatly assert that they are, then decency, thoughtfulness and the likes of attentive listening should know no peers in the management canon.

*Tom Peters*

**Realism**

Where you stand depends on where you sit.

*Rufus Miles*

The future ain't what it used to be.

*Yogi Berra*

Those who gossip to you will also gossip about you.

*John Hagee*

Wisdom comes from facing the wind; fools let it carry them.

*Daniel Boone*

Whatever the role of government in stabilizing our economy with stimulus packages or changing regulation and supervision, it will be the private sector and private enterprise that lead us out of this.

*Tony Blair*

Only through defeat is character built.

*Tom Landry*

You are only as successful as the people who work for you want you to be.

*Leonard Lauder*

Fill what's empty; empty what's full.

*Alice Roosevelt Longworth*

We have become too apologetic, too feeble, too inhibited, too infused with doubt, and too lacking in mission. Our way of life, our values, the things that make us great, remain not simply as a testament to us as a great nation but as a harbinger of human progress.

*Tony Blair*

Too often, life takes over and pushes experiences that might enrich, enlarge, and even complete us, to the bottom of our to-do list.

*Lee Kravitz*

British newspapers: they are rarely genuine and they are for the most part extremely misrepresentative, often through ignorance, often through design, and, very frequently, the whole is a mere matter of invention.

*Sir Edmund Burke*

Socialism works until you run out of other people's money.

*Margaret Thatcher*

The problem is the same in every gold rush: the gold is easier to sell than to mine.

*Lindsey Conner*

The fewer the number, the greater the honor.

*William Shakespeare*

Do what you love, love what you do.

*Deion Sanders*

Grief is the price to be paid for love.

*Queen Elizabeth, the Queen Mother*

Turning conservative after a crisis is like closing the barn door after the horse has left.

*Howard Marks*

If you can't explain what you're doing in plain English, you're probably doing something wrong.

*Alfred E. Kahn*

A lie gets around the world 30 times before the truth even gets its boots on.

*Donald Rumsfeld*

If people aren't secure enough in their own being, they can't camouflage it.

*Paul Celle*

Chasing popularity is a fleeting moment; operating on principals lasts forever.

*George W. Bush*

Social pain is a type of injury. To ease it, reach out to friends and family.

*Nancy Comiskey*

Leaders not only need a strong backbone but also a great funny bone.

*Elizabeth Dole*

The gift of listening trumps the gift of gab.

*Kurt Mortensen*

If it comes easy to you, imagine what you could give if you dug a little deeper.

*Quang Ho*

Smart training, building resilient attitudes and developing a better working relationship with fear can help us achieve true grace under pressure.

*Taylor Clark*

Good for all of us in the trying times we are going through, to consider those early days, when the problems were even greater, and learn the lessons which the characters of the men who founded the United States have to teach us.

*Eleanor Roosevelt*

Time is the greatest and most precious nonrenewable resource – so use it wisely. Once it's gone you can't get it back.

*Shayna N. Stonom*

Overconsumption of anything can lead to negative effects.

*Amanda Smith*

There are too many pigs for the teats.

*Abraham Lincoln*

Freedom is never more than one generation away from extinction. We didn't pass it to our children in the bloodstream. It must be fought for, protected, and handed on for them to do the same.

*Ronald Reagan*

If you have a job without any aggravations, you don't have a job.

*Malcolm Forbes*

We all want to be special, to stand out; there's nothing wrong with this. The irony is that every human being is special to start with. But we then go through some sort of boot camp from the age of zero to eighteen where we learn everything we can about how not to be unique.

*Karl Marlantes*

Everything in this life is on loan.

*Giovanni Agnelli*

Lying to yourself or being less than honest with yourself messes up your brain and can cause problems all your life.

*Don Hodges*

Find a passion outside your job. If you're lucky enough to have a career you love, it can be hard to remember to find a hobby you love just as much. But find that hobby and invest in it, whether it's golf, swing dancing, or community theater. Find something that is a source of enrichment in your life – and make time for it.

*John Baldoni*

Scientists have documented the health benefits of staying in a long-term romantic relationship, including reduced illness and longer life. Employees who stick with a single company rather than job-hop tend for the most part to be better compensated financially and to be more productive and creative, other research has found. Another study shows that continuing to root for one's hometown team helps ease the anxiety of moving to a new city.

*Shirley Wang*

Saying what you think is not always good diplomacy, but it serves you well in the long run.

*Don Hodges*

Giving a helping hand in the long term is more satisfying that receiving a helping hand.

*Don Hodges*

Before anyone is given unemployment insurance, they should be forced to take a drug test.

*Gary Hodges*

One of the great things about America is that you get a second chance, and some of us need it.

*Dick Cheney*

A fanatic is one who can't change his mind and won't change the subject.

*Winston Churchill*

A trust pact is a family's best asset and if broken it takes a long time to win it back.

*Camille Hodges Hays*

If it looks too good to be true, it probably is.

*Dr. L. Jack Bolton*

What life brings to you has already been chosen for you. But what you bring to life is your choice. Life happens, that's a given. But how your life turns out is up to you. You can make it what you want.

*Shayna N. Stonom*

Don't lose touch with reality.

*Rolf Haberecht*

# Business

**Tim Cox,** *Silver Charm*

Any successful business will provide a service or a product that other people want or need. There is a selfish element in business, but the altruistic part is greater; it is the fulcrum for success. If you offer a needed, wanted product or service, and deliver it in an altruistic manner, you will have happy clientele. And happy customers lead to business success.

Certainly, any business demands careful thought, planning and discipline, in addition to great leadership, employees and assistance to execute properly. But a giving, cheerful attitude will tilt the balance in your favor every time.

All I can say is beware of geeks bearing formulas.'

*Warren Buffett*

Never do business with anyone you can't trust.

*J.P. Morgan*

Corporate indebtedness is like a dagger tied to the steering wheel of your car pointed at your heart. You will someday hit a pothole.

*Warren Buffet*

In a difficult business, no sooner is one problem solved than another surfaces. Never is there just one cockroach in the kitchen. Overall, we've done better by avoiding dragons than by slaying them.

*Warren Buffet*

Some companies are prisoners of their point of view.

*Steve Jobs*

There is only one valid definition of business purpose: to create a customer. The customer is the foundation of a business and keeps it in existence.

*Peter F. Drucker*

There's never been a company that's filed for bankruptcy that had no debt.

*Peter Lynch*

Take care of your employees; they'll take care of your customers.

*J. Willard Marriott*

The simple problem of our age is how to act decisively in the absence of certainty.

*Bertrand Russell*

There is no advertising as potent as a satisfied customer.

*Stanley Marcus*

**Horse Sense. Street Smarts.**

Pick an industry that you're really infatuated with and think has a great future, learn that industry and then look for unexplored opportunities.

*Ross Perot*

The buyer is entitled to a bargain. The seller is entitled to a profit. So there is a fine margin in between where the price is right.

*Conrad Hilton*

The conduct of successful business merely consists in doing things in a very simple way, doing them regularly, and never neglecting to do them.

*William Hesketh Lever*

You can't make all good deals in business. What you've got to do is make more good deals than bad deals.

*Alan Bond*

Good managements are like cats. If they fall out of a window, they have a tendency to land on their feet.

*Bill Sams*

Forecasting is always risky business, particularly if it happens to be about the future.

*Sam Goldwyn*

When buying companies or common stock, we look for first class businesses accompanied by first class management. I learned to go into business only with people whom I like, trust and admire. We do not wish to join with managers who lack admirable qualities, no matter how attractive the prospects of their business. We've never succeeded in making a good deal with a bad person.

*Warren Buffet*

Good is not an option; it has to be exceptional. This philosophy is a good one for every business.

*Wolfgang Puck*

Apart from the ballot box, philanthropy presents the one opportunity the individual has to express his meaningful choice over the direction in which our society will progress.

*George G. Kirsten*

Invest in successful companies, not problem companies.

*Carlton G. Lutts*

Great companies are built in tough times.

*James Morgan*

People are the important part of any business.

*Richard Perkins*

There's no such thing as a bad idea. Maybe there are ideas that don't work. Maybe there are ideas that we won't accept. But we want to hear them.

*Andrew J. Higgins*

Leadership is a matter of having people look at you and gain confidence, seeing how you react. If you're in control, they're in control. If you want to see me as a cheerleader, that would mean I was only watching instead of thinking.

*Tom Landry*

As in the nature of things, those which most admirably flourish, most swiftly fester or putrefy, as roses, lilies, violets, while others last; so in the lives of men, those that are most blooming, are soonest turned into the opposite.

*Pliny the Elder*

Sometimes the best deals you do are the deals you don't do.

*Jim Edson*

Know the value of planned abandonment...you must decide what not to do.

*Peter Drucker*

**Horse Sense. Street Smarts.**

Goods are traded, but services are consumed and produced in the same place.

*Thomas L. Friedman*

People decisions are the ultimate control mechanism of an organization. That's where people look to find out what values you really hold.

*Peter Drucker*

There exist limitless opportunities in every industry. Where there is an open mind, there will always be a frontier.

*Charles Kettering*

An organization begins to die the day it begins to be run for the benefit of the insiders and not for the benefit of the outsiders.

*Peter Drucker*

Life is too short to be unhappy, so find a place where the company and the employees are both happy. Once the right people are in the right positions, we leave them alone to do their jobs. Find good people and give them more responsibility and authority. You can't micro-manage them. My main function is goal setting. Let people know what your goals are for them, give them the tools to achieve those goals and step back.

*Don Tomnitz*

In sports or business, you need patience. You have to have a blueprint and a plan to follow that's based on experts that are far more capable than you.

*Mark Spitz*

If you weren't already in a business would you enter it today? If the answer is no, what are you going to do about it?

*Peter Drucker*

When you have managers of high character running businesses about which they are passionate, you can have a dozen or more reporting to you and still have time for an afternoon nap. Conversely, if you have one person reporting to you who is deceitful, inept, or uninterested, you will find yourself with more than you can handle.

*Warren Buffett*

Don't ever take a job because of the prestige of the title or the amount of the paycheck.

*Colleen Barrett*

Quality drives quantity.

*Leslie Wexner*

I early found that when I worked for myself alone, myself alone worked for me, but when I worked for others, others worked for me.

*Benjamin Franklin*

A successful job applicant is not someone who simply needs a job, but someone who can solve an employer's problems.

*Virginia Postrel*

Management is doing things right; leadership is doing the right things.

*Peter Drucker*

Building a program is a long-term thing—you're going to have times when you take two steps forward and maybe take one step back.

*Greg Brohm*

Look at the business from a long term perspective and don't cut corners for short term gain. Always run to where the ball is going, not where it is, and most importantly, play your game.

*Bernay Box*

Company managements are liars, bull shooters, or honest people giving optimistic predictions. They are frequently the last to recognize a problem.

*Anonymous*

Leadership is defining the truth.

*Pat Riley*

Chance favors the prepared mind.

*Louis Pasteur*

When you can work well with other human beings, it's more than just a great business strategy; it's also a great way to build a well rounded and fulfilling life. It's something you can take home with you.

*John Bogle*

CEOs are the keepers of the values of their organization, a single beacon alone is not sufficient illumination but the absence of this one beacon can undercut all others.

*Rick Teerlink*

If we cannot do business by fair and square methods, we prefer not to do business at all.

*William Wrigley*

There are times when the normal rules don't apply. It might be more dangerous to be passive—it can be less risky to take risk.

*George Soros*

Leaders—from Roosevelt to Churchill to Reagan—inspire people with clear visions of how things can be done better. Some managers, on the other hand, muddle things with pointless complexity and detail. They equate (managing) with sophistication, with sounding smarter than anyone else. They inspire no one.

*Jack Welch*

It seems to me more important to read stuff you disagree with than to read stuff you agree with.

*Milton Friedman*

Every time you hear the phrase "everybody else is doing it," it should raise a red flag. Start with what is legal, but always go on to what you would feel comfortable having printed on the front page of the local newspaper.

*Warren Buffett*

In business, you reward people for taking risks. When it doesn't work out, you promote them because you were willing to try new things. If people come back and tell me they skied all day and never fell down, I tell them to try a different mountain. I have always joked that the difference between having the courage of your convictions and being pigheaded is in the results.

*Michael Bloomberg*

Bad times can be good for your business—if you're ready for them.

*Sandy Weill*

When negotiating a deal, tell your rival what you want the moment you sit down at the negotiating table. It gets the deal done faster. You totally disarm them by putting your cards out on the table. You take all the cleverness out of the game.

*Jack Welch*

The Holy Grail is not top line sales growth. It's bottom line growth.

*Jim Owens*

When we are debating an issue, loyalty means giving me your honest opinion, whether you think I'll like it or not. Disagreement at this stage stimulates me. But once a decision has been made, the debate ends. From that point on, loyalty means executing the decision as if it were your own.

*Colin Powell*

I don't believe you can effectively manage people without helping them understand where they fit into the goals of the organization.

*Tom Landry*

The five most dangerous words in business are: everybody else is doing it.

*Warren Buffett*

An institution is in trouble when its memories of the past are greater than its hope for the future.

*Robert Jeffress*

Successful entrepreneurs do not wait until the muse kisses them and gives them a bright idea; they go to work.

*Peter F. Drucker*

Those entrepreneurs who start out with the idea that they'll make it big and in a hurry can be guaranteed failure.

*Peter F. Drucker*

I have seen many downturns in business. Always, America has emerged from these stronger and more prosperous.

*Thomas Edison*

Have the discipline to say no and the patience to wait for the right opportunity; make decisions when no one agrees with you and take advantage of other's fear and greed. And be a prolific reader of the financial press.

*Mason Hawkins*

By taking prosperity for granted, people perversely subvert prosperity. The more business managers, investors, consumers think that economic growth is guaranteed and that risk and uncertainty are receding, the more we act in ways that raise risk, magnify uncertainty, and threaten economic growth. Prosperity destabilizes itself.

*Robert J. Samuelson*

I think a lot of good companies make their worst mistakes in the best of times.

*Jim Owens*

We look for people who can work well together, that complement the team. I focus on helping people understand the goals, the vision, what we could be, the realities of where we are, and what we need to do to improve and get ourselves to the next level.

*Jim Owens*

Organizations don't really accomplish anything. Theories of management don't much matter. Endeavors succeed or fail because of the people involved. Only by attracting the best people will you accomplish great things.

*Hyman Rickover*

Too often executives and managers stay in their offices and behind their desks. They may hear of conditions in the organizations they lead, but they do not see these conditions for themselves firsthand. Yet there is no substitute for firsthand information and direct contact.

*Alan Axelrod*

This, then, is my thesis: I firmly believe that any organization, in order to survive and achieve success, must have a sound set of beliefs on which it premises all its policies and actions. Next, I believe that the most important single factor in corporate success is faithful adherence to those beliefs. And, finally, I believe that if an organization is to meet the challenges of a changing world, it must be prepared to change everything about itself except those beliefs as it moves through corporate life.

*Thomas Watson, Jr.*

When you buy bad companies, they are always worse than you thought.

*Anders Scharp*

Whilst debt is good for raising equity returns, any business or acquisition that is over leveraged is invariably headed for failure.

*Abdul Rahman Ahmad*

Speaking of a lawsuit in which Mary Crowley was being interrogated, cited a point at which an attorney for the other side asked her if it were true that a good salesman could sell anything. Her answer, which surprised the attorney, was, No! A good salesman can only sell something he believes in. He further quoted her as saying, on many occasions, she would rather have one believer than ninety nine who were interested.

*Doug Atkins*

You have to follow your brain when it tells you to do something.

*Granville Lassater*

Don't tell me what we can make on a deal. What can we lose?

*Sir Gordon White*

The person with the superior knowledge of the wares, be he buyer or seller, has the decided advantage.

*Dean Krakel*

People leave companies like T.I., start new companies and create the next wave of innovation.

*Phil Ritter*

It's the plan we use at our company: God, first. Family, second. Company, third. And Sales, fourth.

*Bo Pilgrim*

Quality is the best kind of advertising in the world.

*Milton Hershey*

Innovation in management is adaptive. Management is not a science, like physics, with immutable laws and testable theories. Management, at its best, is an intelligent response to outside forces, often disruptive ones.

*Steve Lohr*

Government control isn't the answer or Russia would have won the cold war.

*Steve Forbes*

Perhaps it is worthwhile to emphasize again the fact that it is not merely capital and plants and the strictly material things which make up a business, but the character of the men behind these things, their personalities and their abilities: these are the essentials to be reckoned with.

*John D. Rockefeller, Sr.*

When prices are high, people in our industry get the easy glow and do things they regret a few years later. One of our strengths is that we try to look through the cycle and avoid both the easy glow and the easy glum.

*Lee Raymond*

Whenever profits and wealth and creativity are denigrated in society, they start to disappear—leaving everyone the poorer.

*Stephen Moore*

You can't retain employees if you don't spread credit around.

*Albert Gordon*

Far too many people in business are interested in their quarter-by-quarter earnings rather than thinking about where the institution is going several years out. I think to be successful, a business manager has to spend a lot of time thinking about the future and how the structure of the organization needs to be changed to cope with the future.

*David Rockefeller*

When you hire someone, you look for brains, energy and integrity, and, if you don't have the third, integrity, you better watch out, because the first two will kill you.

*Warren Buffett*

**Horse Sense. Street Smarts.**

Book value is a conservative but reasonably accurate proxy for growth in intrinsic business value, the measurement that really counts.

*Warren Buffett*

A new CEO can't turn around a company alone. He has to get a buy-in from employees and the board. That's a big part of being a successful CEO.

*Les Funtleyder*

When a management team with a reputation for brilliance tackles a business with a reputation for bad economics, it's the reputation of the business that remains intact.

*Warren Buffett*

Screw it, let's do it.

*Richard Branson*

I think that business has a noble purpose. It's not that there's anything wrong with making money. It's one of the important things that business contributes to society. But it's not the sole reason that business exists.

*John Mackey*

We need not apologize for being zealous advocates for our clients.

*Michael Richardson*

I have two requirements before I hire someone—no. 1, they're smart, and no. 2, they work hard.

*Boone Pickens*

Be realistic; gauge how many challenges are created by the economy, and how many are self-inflicted. Assess your situation, how long the downturn will last and how deep it will be. It usually is longer than you think. Get ready for the upturn and get closer to your customers.

*John Chambers*

The purpose of any business is to create and keep a customer.

*Peter Drucker*

If you have to do a lot of math to find out if you're going to make a profit, then it's probably not worth it.

*Charlie Munger*

Protect the downside.

*Richard Branson*

Economic difficulties are a time when companies can reassess where they are in the market and rebuild themselves rapidly.

*Michael Dell*

Companies that master the delicate balance between cutting costs to survive today, and investing to grow tomorrow do well after a recession.

*Franz Wohlgezogen*

Everyone gets the same information at basically the same time, so the value of information has gone to zero. And there has not been proportionate growth in the investment community's ability to sort through it all. People spend so much time absorbing that they don't have time to understand what it means. That's why the value of expertise and the ability to interpret information will someday go to infinity.

*Wilbur Ross*

Speed, for me, is everything—in decision-making, in execution, in reacting, it's the most important differential

*Roger Agnelli*

Treat your customers as friends. Simply put, if they like you, they'll buy from you; if they don't, they won't.

*Dennis Hull*

**Horse Sense. Street Smarts.**

The number one thing people want from their employers: respect.

*Mihaly Csikszentmihalyi*

When positive groupthink permeates an organization, naysayers are marginalized and realities are overlooked. That's why promotion-focused organizations are often blind sided by poor financial results.

*Ranjay Gulati*

Take bad news as an opportunity to turn failures into concrete improvements. Examine customer complaints more often than company financials.

*Bill Gates*

A focus solely on cost-cutting causes several problems. First, executives and employees start approaching every decision through a loss-minimizing lens. Second, instead of learning to operate more efficiently, the organization tries to do more of the same with less. That often results in lower quality and a drop in customer satisfaction.

*Nitin Nohria*

The bigger the prize people are chasing, the more people go after it. As people pile into the area, the expected returns to anyone investor go down. Yet the returns to society go up.

*Paul Romer*

Having a fortress balance sheet was a strategic imperative for us during the good times, because we knew that sooner or later a crisis would hit.

*Jamie Dimon*

So much is said about fair market value with few even knowing what fair market value is. I believe the legal definition is a willing buyer and willing seller, neither being under any compulsion to buy or sell and both having knowledge of relevant facts.'

*Doug Singleton*

In business, you can change human behavior by incentives, not sermons.

*Warren Buffett*

Imitation is under appreciated. It can be more important to business growth than innovation. Imitation is not mindless repetition: it's an intelligent search for cause and effect.

*Oded Shenkar*

Nobody can predict interest rates, the future direction of the economy, or the stock market. Dismiss all such forecasts and concentrate on what's actually happening.

*Peter Lynch*

If you take care of your customers, take care of your associates, the stock will take care of itself.

*Bernie Marcus*

When you decide, you divide.

*Tony Blair*

Most businesses change in character and quality over the years, sometimes for the better, perhaps more often for the worse.

*Benjamin Graham*

Entrepreneurs have a high tolerance for risk. Thus their own perception of the odds they're facing doesn't always square with the grim reality of the situation, which explains why they drive forward where more cautious souls would not.

*Boone Pickens*

Innovation thrives when ideas can serendipitously connect and combine with other ideas. A great deal of the past two centuries of legal and folk wisdom about innovation has pursued the exact opposite argument, building walls between ideas. These walls keep ideas sequestered, reducing the overall network of minds that can potentially engage with a problem.

*Steven Johnson*

I love NASCAR. It is a kind of metaphor for business. It is about execution, speed, precision, and teamwork, which is not unlike running a company. It is also a sport in which you have to tolerate fan criticism. But most of all, it's a precision sport and winning is all about execution.

*Robert Nardelli*

Accept that people may not do them quite the same way you do, but that does not mean they are doing them badly.

*Leonard Lauder*

You can't give feedback to clients in anything but a constructive fashion. You can't just push back willy-nilly, and you don't win arguments with clients, period. If you aren't being audacious, if you aren't challenging, if you aren't pushing back, you're on your way out the door.

*Romil Bahl*

The hard reality is that market pricing mechanisms are the best way to ration supply. Companies that don't recoup their cost with at least some measure of profit are destined for the dustbin.

*Benjamin Shepherd*

The law of supply and demand governs the prices of just about everything in life, whether it be tomatoes or stocks. If there is short supply and big demand, you can count on high prices. But if there's an abundance of supply and limited demand, prices will be low.

*Vincent Mao*

Do the right thing and always encourage others to do right, honest and ethical things.

*Jim Wright*

## Minding the Store

It's up to management to decide if any item should sell, not whether it will sell.

There is never a good sale for Neiman Marcus unless it's a good buy for the customer.

There is the right customer for every piece of merchandise, his father told him, and it was the merchant's job not only to bring the two pieces together but also to prevent the customer from making the wrong choice.

I found that when I took care of customers extremely well, and made them the focal point, profit inevitably flowed from that.

Quality is remembered long after price is forgotten. If you force a bad buy on a customer, he will never forgive you.

When Marcus learned of a dissatisfied customer, he'd contact him immediately.

*Stanley Marcus*
*(From an article in* Investor's Business Daily*)*

Most cycles in business follow the same principle we learn in physics: once a pendulum has reached the limit of its force, gravity takes over and returns it to equilibrium.

*Robert W. Decherd*

Most cycles in business follow the same principle we learn in physics: once a pendulum has reached the limit of its force, gravity takes over and returns it to equilibrium.

*Robert W. Decherd*

The exercise and activity that you were doing ten years ago determines your condition today. What you are doing today will determine your condition ten years from now.

*Rich Sillman*

The common question asked in business is: why? That's a good question, but an equally valid question is: why not?

*Jeff Bezos*

There is the will to conquer, the impulse to fight, to prove oneself superior, to succeed for the sake not the fruits of success but of success itself. There is the joy of creating, of getting things done, or simply of exercising one's energy and ingenuity.

*The Wall Street Journal*

Keep things informal. Talking is the natural way to do business. Writing is great for keeping records and putting down details, but talk generates ideas. Great things come from our luncheon meetings, which consist of a sandwich, a cup of soup, and a good idea or two. No martinis.

*Boone Pickens*

There are two times when you should evaluate your sales organization. Number one when business is down and number two when business is good.

*Jack Hutchison*

The culture of a company is like the sand on a beach. Wind and water are always eroding it. It's the job of leadership to replenish the culture one grain at a time, all the time.

*Jim Wright*

All of the hula hoops haven't been invented.

*Gary Boren*

Every time you hear a new word, look it up and use it in a sentence.

*Camille Hodges Hays*

**Horse Sense. Street Smarts.**

# Faith

**Tim Cox, *Where the Sun Shines***

L ife is much more than what we can see with our own eyes on day-to-day basis. To successfully survive the ups and downs of life (and we all have them), one must be anchored to a belief in divine providence. We are not here on earth by accident. We are here for a purpose.

Faith in something greater than ourselves allows us to consider others first, to be kind to others, to help others and to realize that we are all merely fragile flesh and blood human beings. Faith in a supreme being to guide and direct us is fundamental to a good life, both personally and professionally.

But when you give a banquet, invite the poor, the crippled, the lame, the blind, and you will be blessed.

*Luke 14:13-14*

Therefore everyone who hears these words of mine and puts them into practice is like a wise man who built his house on the rock. The rain came down, the streams rose, and the winds blew and beat against that house; yet it did not fall, because it had its foundation on the rock. But everyone who hears these words of mine and does not put them into practice is like a foolish man who built his house on sand. The rain came down, the streams rose, and the winds blew and beat against that house, and it fell with a great crash.

*Matthew 7:24-27*

Science cannot disprove the existence of God.

*Richard P. Feynman*

This is a transitory world; all things here must perish with their using, but there are substantial riches in heaven prepared by God through the blood of Christ. May I not hope that you will embrace him with your whole heart?

*H. G. Blake*

Commit your work to the Lord, then it will succeed.

*Proverbs 16:3*

Purely rational thinking can lead you only so far. There comes a time when you have the leap and trust your intuition.

*Malcolm Westcott*

Trust in your money and down you go. Trust in God and flourish like a tree.

*Proverbs 11:28*

Failure is never final. God specializes in restoration, it is His best work.

*Ruth Graham*

God has a plan, even when you don't understand it fully. But you do have a sense of it, and you have a choice. You can conduct yourself in accordance with it, or not. You can either do good, or bad.

*Rudy Giuliani*

The secret to getting through the Valley of Death is to keep on walking.

*Darrell Cain, Sr.*

You cannot arrive at your life's purpose by starting with a focus on yourself. You must begin with God, your creator. You exist only because God wills that you exist. You were made by God, for God and until you understand that, life will never make sense. It is only in God that we find our origin, our identity, our meaning, our purpose, our significance, and our destiny. Every other path leads to a dead-end.

*Rick Warren*

Coincidences are the best way for God to establish a perpetual presence in your life.

*Squire Rushnell*

Whatever you do, work at it with all your heart, as working for the Lord not for men, since you know that you will receive an inheritance from the Lord as a reward. It is the Lord Christ you are serving.

*Colossians 3:23-24*

The secret to everything is to let yourself be carried by the Lord and to carry the Lord.

*Pope John XXIII*

I realized I couldn't ask for God's help while at the same time I felt hatred for the mixed up young man who had shot me. Isn't that the meaning of the lost sheep? We are all God's children and therefore equally loved by him.

*Ronald Reagan*

If you don't confess your sins, you will be a failure. But God will be merciful if you confess your sins and give them up.

*Proverbs 28:13*

Gold and silver are tested in a red-hot furnace, but we are tested by praise.

*Proverbs 27:21*

Having accepted Jesus Christ as my Savior, I have God's promise of eternal life in Heaven, as well as abundant life here on earth that he promises to each of us in John 10:10.

*Ronald Reagan*

Trust God

*Proverbs 3:1-4*

My child, remember my teachings and instructions and obey them completely. They will help you live a long and prosperous life. Let love and loyalty always show like a necklace, and write them in your mind. God and people will like you and consider you a success.

*Proverbs 3:1-4*

Trust in your wealth, and you will be a failure, but God's people will prosper like healthy plants.

*Proverbs 11:28*

We humans make plans, but the Lord has the final word.

*Proverbs 16:1*

Without risk, faith is impossibility.

*Soren Kierkegaard*

Pray now, pray often, pray much—it is the only way. Press on—keep looking up.

*Gil Stricklin*

I don't see how anyone could not believe in God.

*Oliver Hodges*

If you wander from the Lord and commit sin, just remember to come back to the Lord.

*William H. Atkinson*

It is impossible to rightly govern the world without God and the Bible.

*George Washington*

Without God there is no virtue because there is no prompting of the conscience...without God there is a coarsening of the society; without God democracy will not and cannot long endure. If we ever forget that we are One Nation under God, then we will be a Nation gone under.

*Ronald Reagan*

The omniscient Lord of the universe doesn't need juries and due process. He knows every sin we've committed. When we confess our sins to this Judge, he declares us not innocent but pardoned.

*Dr. James C. Denison*

By this all men will know that you are my disciples, if you love one another.

*John 13:35*

We make a living by what we get; we make a life by what we give.

*Ronald Reagan*

## How Proverbs Can Be Used

1.  These are the proverbs of King Solomon of Israel, the son of David.

2.  Proverbs will teach you wisdom and self-control and how to understand sayings with deep meanings.

3.  You will learn what is right and honest and fair.

4.  From these, an ordinary person can learn to be clever, and young people can gain knowledge and good sense.

5.  If you are already wise, you will become even wiser. And if you are clever, you will learn to understand

6.  proverbs and sayings, as well as words of wisdom and all kinds of riddles.

7.  Respect and obey the LORD! This is the beginning of knowledge. Only a fool rejects wisdom and good advice. Warnings against bad friends

8.  My child, obey the teachings of your parents,

9.  and wear their teachings as you would a lovely hat or a pretty necklace.

10. Don't be tempted by sinners or listen

11. when they say, "Come on! Let's gang up and kill somebody, just for the fun of it!

12. They're well and healthy now, but we'll finish them off once and for all.

13. We'll take their valuables and fill our homes with stolen goods.

14. If you join our gang, you'll get your share."

15. Don't follow anyone like that or do what they do.

16. They are in a big hurry to commit some crime, perhaps even murder.

17. They are like a bird that sees the bait, but ignores the trap.

18. They gang up to murder someone, but they are the victims.

**Horse Sense. Street Smarts.**

19.  The wealth you get from crime robs you of your life.

### Wisdom Speaks

20.  Wisdom shouts in the streets wherever crowds gather.

21.  She shouts in the market places and near the city gates as she says to the people,

22.  "How much longer will you enjoy being stupid fools? Won't you ever stop sneering and laughing at knowledge?

23.  Listen as I correct you and tell you what I think.

24.  You completely ignored me and refused to listen;

25.  you rejected my advice and paid no attention when I warned you.

26.  "So when you are struck by some terrible disaster,

27.  or when trouble and distress surround you like a whirlwind, I will laugh and make fun of you.

28.  You will ask for my help, but I won't listen; you will search, but you won't find me.

29.  No, you would not learn, and you refused to respect the LORD.

30.  You rejected my advice and paid no attention when I warned you.

31.  "Now you will eat the fruit of what you have done, until you are stuffed full with your own schemes.

32.  Sin and self-satisfaction bring destruction and death to stupid fools.

33.  But if you listen to me, you will be safe and secure without fear of disaster."

*Proverbs 1:1-33*

Do all you can and trust the outcome to God.

*Capt. Arthur W. Peterson*

To educate a man in mind and not in morals is to educate a menace to society."

*Teddy Roosevelt*

The Church is a hospital for sinners, not a museum for saints.

*Dr. Robert Schuller*

A wise man reads the Book of Proverbs at least once a year.

*Dr. L. Jack Bolton*

**Horse Sense. Street Smarts.**

# Humor

**Tim Cox,** *The Swimmin' Hole*

Humor has a very special place in the business world. Use it in a thoughtful manner, and it can help you rise above the herd. Use it improperly, and you might be set up for a fall. There are times that even Will Rogers could not have influenced a grin. Good old-fashioned horse sense plays a big part in what to say and when. If you have a customer smiling after an encounter, you know you have used your sense of humor wisely.

White House occupants come and go. They are just like diapers. They should be changed often, and for the same reason.

*Paul Harvey*

Predictions are hard to make, especially when they concern the future.

*Yogi Berra*

We are all ignorant, just about different things.

*Will Rogers*

If you put the federal government in charge of the Sahara Desert, in five years, there'd be a shortage of sand.

*Milton Friedman*

A committee is a group of people who get together to share their ignorance.

*Judge James Harrod*

Never give the devil a ride; he'll always want to drive.

*Nadine*

Everyone has the brain power to make money in stocks. Not everyone has the stomach.

*Peter Lynch*

Politics is supposed to be the second oldest profession. I have come to realize that it bears a very close resemblance to the first.

*Ronald Reagan*

Being 100% invested when the market is in a serious decline is like being caught naked with no clothes in sight.

*Don Hodges*

Most politicians could not run a lemonade stand.

*Bernie Goldberg*

As an attorney, it's expected that you'll have to argue your point. But don't be a jerk about it.

*Kevin Sullivan*

I don't like to be the guy in church who coughs loudly just before putting money into the offering plate.

*John Wooden*

That money talks I can't deny. I heard it once, it said goodbye.

*Dee Miller*

**Horse Sense. Street Smarts.**

# Money

**Tim Cox,** *Rumbling Thunder*

The right use, the wrong use and even the abuse of money is something that's been going on throughout history. Money can be a tool for good or the seed for a personal downfall.

One thing is certain; it should always be handled carefully and thoughtfully. Learning how to handle the reins early can enhance one's life significantly.

Anytime you have an economy where people are suddenly looking for cash, then all assets are going to depreciate in relation to money.

*Don Hodges*

Buy the finest home you can afford and the worst auto you can tolerate.

*Charles Liu*

Prosperity consists of getting more and more narrow in what you make, and more and more diverse in what you buy.

*Matt Ridley*

Don't do this to become a millionaire; money is the wrong motivation. Do this for passion and the money will follow.

*Julio Palmaz*

A just price is simply what goods are worth according to the estimation of the market at the time of the sale.

*Albertus Magnus*

Avoiding big mistakes is key to generating long term wealth.

*Don Phillip*

We think much more about the use of money, which is renewable, than we do about the use of our time, which is irreplaceable.

*Peter Lynch*

Beware of little expenses; a small leak will sink a great ship.

*Benjamin Franklin*

Sell good merchandise at a reasonable profit, treat your customers/ clients like human beings, and they'll always come back for more.

*L.L. Bean*

Buy what thou hast no need of and ere long thou shall sell thy necessaries.

*Benjamin Franklin*

**Horse Sense. Street Smarts.**

Older people regularly practice the virtue of thrift when it does nothing but demonstrate the virtue. The young, meanwhile, spend. This is precisely the reverse of what makes sense. A dollar saved at age 25 is worth $4.00 saved at age 43; $8.00 saved at age 52, and $16.00 put aside at age 61.

*Scott Burns (1989)*

Real estate is not easy to get out of; consequently, people stay in and build fortunes.

*Bill Berger*

Maximizing profits is the noblest social goal a company can have.

*Milton Friedman*

Worried money never wins.

*John Dessauer*

He who has a thing to sell and goes and whispers in a well, is not so apt to get the dollars as he who climbs a tree and hollers.

*Anonymous*

The thrifty will eventually own the spendthrifts.

*Sir John Templeton*

Capitalistic countries grow on debt.

*Bill Berger*

A wise man saveth for the future, but the foolish man spends whatever he gets.

*Proverbs 21:20*

Just as the rich rule the poor, so the borrower is servant of the lender.

*Proverbs 22:7*

Trying to get rich is evil and leads to poverty.

*Proverbs 29:22*

No money—no life.

*Chinese Proverb*

When it gets too easy to make money, get out of the way.

*Roger Lipton*

My idea has been to get out of debt as soon as you can and keep down expenses. It's a simple country man's philosophy, but it works.

*Edward Ball*

If you're gonna play the game, boy, you gotta learn to play it right. You've got to know when to hold'em, know when to fold' em. Know when to walk away, know when to run. You never count your money when you're sittin' at the table. There'll be time enough for countin' when the dealin's done. Every gambler knows that the secret to survivin' is knowin' what to throwaway and knowin' what to keep. Cause every hand's a winner and every hand's a loser.

*Don Schlitz (Excerpt from* The Gambler*)*

Borrowing money to fund losses is a little like heating your house by throwing the furniture in the fireplace. It's not a long-term strategy.

*Thomas Horton*

If it's in the papers, it's in the price.

*Bill Miller*

I don't want to become possessed by my possessions.

*Laurence Tisch*

Managing earnings: The process has little to do with running a business and the numbers can become distractingly and dangerously detached from fundamentals.

*Barry Diller*

Wealthy people do not want to make 50%; they just don't want to lose 10%.

*Richard Fisher*

The real measure of our wealth is how much we would be worth if we lost all our money!

*The Wall Street Journal*

My father said it's alright to gamble, but don't ever try to get even. Lose what you can afford to lose, and then leave the table. You can lose it all trying to double up to catch up.

*Bunker Hunt*

I ain't as much interested in the return on my money, as the return of my money.

*Will Rogers*

I do not keep money to look at.

*George Washington*

All that can be required of the trustee to invest, is, that he should conduct himself faithfully and exercise a sound discretion. He is to observe how men of prudence, discretion and intelligence manage their own affairs, not in regard to speculation, but in regard to the permanent disposition of their funds, considering the probable income, as well as the probable safety of the capital to be invested.

*Samuel Putman*

It is the part of a wise man to keep himself today for tomorrow, and not to venture all his eggs in one basket.

*Cervantes, Don Quixote*

History tells us that when we become overenthusiastic about certain types of financial arrangements, we overdo it.

*Alan Greenspan*

If you can't pay for a thing, don't buy it. If you can't get paid for it, don't sell it.

*Benjamin Franklin*

The assets may shrink but the debt doesn't.

Gretchen Morgenson

Accumulation is never done to the accompaniment of a brass band.

Charles H. Dow

Companies with too much debt are like humans with a weak immune system; they catch every debilitating thing that comes along.

Don Hodges

If you buy an apartment or a farm, you don't worry about what it's worth today.

Warren Buffett

Wealth is like an orchard. You have to share the fruit, not the trees.

Carlos Slim Helu

When you leave your children a company, you are leaving them a big responsibility and a commitment. You don't want to leave them with money; you want to leave them with a commitment.

Carlos Slim Helu

When you first make money, you may be tempted to spend it. Don't...instead, reinvest the profits.

Warren Buffett

Debt is not a sin, but it is dangerous.

John Hagee

Neither a borrower nor lender be; for loan oft loses both itself and friend, and borrowing dulls the edge of husbandry.

William Shakespeare

It's basic, but still unlearned: human beings must have savings. This is not just a good idea. It's the difference between life and death, terror and calm. So start saving right now and don't stop until you die.

Ben Stein

The Lord shall open unto thee his good treasure, the heaven to give the rain unto thy land in his season, and to bless all the work of thy hand: and thou shalt lend unto many nations and thou shalt not borrow.

*Deuteronomy 28: 12*

Poverty is good for preservation.

*Anonymous*

Every sudden explosion of wealth in a capitalistic society has been accompanied by an explosion of real estate development; nothing is more natural than new castles for the newly rich.

*Thomas G. Donlan*

Credit derivatives arose not from the needs of investors, but from the needs of investment banks.

*Israel Nelken*

The companies in trouble are usually the ones that owe a lot of money.

*Walter Schloss*

Annual income twenty pounds, annual expenditure nineteen six, result happiness. Annual income twenty pounds, annual expenditure twenty pounds ought and six, result misery.

*Charles Dickens*

It's a dangerous thing to guarantee payment for someone's debts. Don't do it!

*Proverbs 11:15*

A boom requires constant infusions of new money to keep going. When the money stops flowing, the boom collapses.

*Doug Stewart*

Real money is Aladdin's lamp.

*Lord Byron*

Since 1929, we've had 4 or 5 recessions and we've learned in this country that we come back.

*Art Linkletter*

A government that robs Peter to pay Paul can always depend on the support of Paul.

*George Bernard Shaw*

Money wrongly gotten will disappear bit by bit; money earned little by little will grow and grow.

*Proverbs 11: 13*

You must remember that you aren't suddenly stupid or inept because you have financial problems. You got caught in a 'perfect storm' of conditions, most of which were beyond your control

*Dr. Phil McGraw*

Free capitalistic societies might develop so great a taste for physical gratification that citizens would be carried away and lose sight of the close connection which exists between the private fortune of each of us and the prosperity of all, and, ultimately, undermine both democracy and prosperity.

*Alexis de Tocqueville*

One common denominator of bubbles is the extreme brevity of financial memory. New generations can buy into the notion that things have changed—that old rules of economics don't apply.

*John Kenneth Galbraith*

The weakening of General Accepted Accounting principles standard over the past 20 years has led to earnings becoming less informative about the true financial health of a business.

*William W. Priest*

The problem with debt is you have to pay it off.

*Don Fitzpatrick*

All crises have involved debt that, in one fashion or another, has become dangerously out of scale in relation to the underlying means of payment.

*John Kenneth Galbraith*

Save 10% of what you make and someday you'll be well off.

*C. R. Anthony*

Frugality doesn't mean doing less. It means doing as much or more with less.

*William S. Marth*

When you're having a good year and making good money, pay some extra on your mortgage.

*Ray Dusek*

Like it or loathe it, the single biggest difference a person can make in life—after your health—is to learn how to look after yourself financially.

*David Eccles*

You can't teach a person high finance who doesn't know how to use a credit card.

*Charlie Munger*

Once the money is acquired, it often disappears as quickly as it comes.

*Tom Dodge*

When times are tough, almost all assets are highly correlated, except for cash. When liquidity dries up, people sell what they can sell, no matter what the price of what they are selling.

*Bruce Berkowitz*

If you ever make a million dollars, don't try to get rich.

*Wayne Cleveland*

Most people go broke because they overspend and tie up too much money in illiquid things.

*Ed Butowsky*

Be on your guard if you borrow to live. For debt will take over with nothing to give.

*Tom Siems*

My father taught me never to have more obligations than you've got coming in.

*Tex Moncrief*

No system can match capitalism in its ability to bring prosperity to so many.

*Investor's Business Daily*

Debt is the foundation of destruction.

*Sarah Palin*

You have to spend money to make money, they always say. They are right, but you also have to keep track of what you spend.

*Caroline Evans*

In buying a home, it's not about how much your monthly payments are, but how quickly you can pay off the mortgage.

*Don Hodges*

The busier we become chasing financial gain, the less likely we are to see clearly and work thoughtfully and to consistently consider the interest of others.

*Margaret Heffernan*

Broke people can't help broke people; only the strong can help the weak.

*Dave Ramsay*

The secret to accumulating wealth and having a comfortable financial existence is to spend less than you make and invest the difference. The earlier you start, the larger the reward.

*Don Hodges*

**Horse Sense. Street Smarts.**

# The Stock Market

**Tim Cox,** *Good Horses and Wide Open Spaces*

Investing is a very broad and complex subject. Stocks are a good or bad investment for a multitude of reasons. Opinions are a dime a dozen and most are misleading and oversimplified. For my money, only a few professional investors possess the experience, through time and activity, to make them worth listening to. The rest can lead you quickly astray.

In this chapter, you will find comments and pointers from some of the best hands in the investment business. Ponder their wisdom, but remember: you make the call.

This is the one thing I can never understand. To refer to a personal taste of mine, I'm going to buy hamburger the rest of my life. When hamburgers go down in price, we sing *Hallelujah Chorus* at the Buffett household. When hamburgers go up, we weep. For most people, it's the same way with everything in life they will be buying – *except* stocks. When stocks go down and you can get more for your money, people don't like them anymore.

*Warren Buffett*

I never have the faintest idea what the stock market is going to do in the next six months, or the next year, or the next two. But I think it is very easy to see what is likely to happen over the long term. Ben Graham told us why: 'Though the stock market functions as a voting machine in the short term, it acts as a weighing machine in the long run.' Fear and greed play important roles when votes are being cast, but they don't register on the scale.

*Warren Buffett*

Why do stocks typically outperform bonds? A major reason is that businesses retain earnings, with these going on to generate still more earnings—and dividends, too.

*Warren Buffett*

The greatest risk is not being invested in stocks.

*Bill Berger*

Since 1920, the market has had forty declines of 10% or more. To be a successful investor, you must understand that it is perfectly natural and provides portfolio managers and investors alike with an investment opportunity. Investors, who fail to recognize this, and instead rely on a short-term outlook, are nearly always disappointed.

*Peter Lynch*

If I make ten investment decisions, three or four will be wrong. The trick is, don't lose too much money when you're wrong.

*Bob Perkins*

**Horse Sense. Street Smarts.**

As long as the market is controlled by humans, the twin emotions of fear and greed will ultimately drive stocks to giddy heights and push them to abysmal lows. It may not be rational, but it is reality.

*attributed to both Peter Lynch & Carlton Lutts*

Market tops do not occur when investors are short-term oriented. They occur when confidence reaches such a point that everyone becomes a long-term investor. By the time the last major top was reached in the market in 1972, they had coined the expression 'one-decision stocks'.

*Street Smart Investor*

If you buy the same securities as other people, you will have the same results as other people.

*Sir John Templeton*

I try never to have a 'position' on the market...that it *should* do this or *should* do that, because that way leads to ego involvement and stubbornness...the deadliest mistake an investment advisor can make. Instead, I always try to follow these two words: stay flexible. That way, I'm ready to move effectively whether the market says go... or whoa.

*Martin E. Zweig*

To be a good investor, it is absolutely imperative to start buying stocks *before* the good news has begun to be prominently displayed. In fact, at every optimum buying opportunity we have seen in two decades, it is almost impossible to find any good news when stocks are either at or close to their eventual lows. That, of course, is the reason they are at their lows.

*Don Hays*

One of the hardest things for investors to grasp is this: the biggest profit potential is not in stocks with good news, but in stocks where the news is bad, but you think likely to get better. That's when the turn for the better is not yet reflected in the price.

*Forbes Magazine, March 17, 1980*

The time of maximum pessimism is the best time to buy, and the time of maximum optimism is the best time to sell. The way to do that is to look at investing differently than you might other activities. The right question to ask is, where is the outlook most miserable?

*Sir John Templeton*

Share prices fluctuate more widely than share values.

*Sir John Templeton*

A lifetime of investment research has taught me to become more and more humble about making predictions.

*Sir John Templeton*

As the bull market endures and highs are followed by still higher highs, and the trader sees the stocks he sold continue to go up, his perception gradually changes. Regardless of how suspect it may be initially, if a condition lasts long enough, one begins to accept it as the norm. The unusual becomes usual; the extraordinary becomes ordinary, and, finally, the unbelievable becomes believable.

It is at this point, where the consensus gives up its nervous short-term orientation and embraces the stock market as the place to be for the long term, that the market is most vulnerable to more than a modest correction.

*Dick Davis*

From my 87 years of experience, there now seems to be a better than even chance that, at the end of this century, the inflation adjusted world standard of living may increase 30-fold and also inflation of world currencies may be 30-fold. In conclusion, at the end of this century, the Standard & Poor's 500 Index may rise 200-fold above today's index.

*Sir John Templeton (April 2000)*

Stock price ultimately follows earnings.

*Bill Berger*

Be invested in the best, most successful companies and you can ride out their performance.

*Bill Berger*

We have always described the investment business in sporting/athletic terms. It has all of the characteristics of the ultimate sport as it demands great mental and physical stamina. It is a contest that has scoring; it has winners and losers; and it has major competitive events each day. It also has divisions to be won or lost; it has a new season each year; and there are teams to be tweaked, changed, motivated and even bought and sold. And, there is the opportunity to be a hero.

*John McStay*

The trend is your friend. In other words, it's no use guessing how long this uptrend of New World stocks will last, or how long the selling of Old World stocks will last. And it's no use telling the market that it's wrong. The market is always right, and once you accept this and learn to listen to it, you'll be a better investor.

*Carlton Lutts*

When companies are perceived as safe investments, that is usually not the case. The best returns come from investments which are perceived to be the most speculative at the time you buy them.

*James L. Fraser*

No one can outsmart the market; you treat the market like you're dancing with a gorilla. If it wants to lead, let it.

*Bill Berger*

To buy when others are despondently selling and to sell when others are greedily buying requires the greatest fortitude and pays the greatest potential reward.

*Sir John Templeton*

Buy value, not market trends or economic outlook.

*Sir John Templeton*

Too many investors focus on outlook and trend. More profit is made by focusing on value.

*Sir John Templeton*

The time to sell an asset is when you have found a much better bargain.

*Sir John Templeton*

In the stock market, the only way to get a bargain is to buy what most investors are selling.

*Sir John Templeton*

Achieving a good investment record is a lot harder than most people think.

*Sir John Templeton*

Often those who buy stocks with borrowed money are later wiped out—forced to sell at just the wrong time. Also, businesses seeking to grow faster than their accumulated savings often borrow too heavily and are later forced into bankruptcy.

*Sir John Templeton*

Don't buy bonds—they have all the risk of stocks and none of the appreciation potential.

*Bill Berger*

Above all, never try to tell the markets what to do. Let them tell you. You'll be glad you did.

*Robert M. Bleiberg*

Uncertainty always makes stocks go down.

*Bill Berger*

You get over-stimulated on Wall Street and you have lots of things that shorten your focus, and a short focus is not conducive to long profits.

*Warren Buffett*

**Horse Sense. Street Smarts.**

To make money in the stock market, you have to learn to be a good loser!

*John Dessauer*

No matter how impressive a company's future, its stock price has to be right to justify a buy or a retention. Wall Street gets carried away by company successes and prices tend to overshoot.

*Dick Strong*

Instead of positive earnings surprises, companies start to report exactly what they said they would. You can see the momentum slowing. We gradually liquidate our position and look for another stock where the cycle is just starting.

*Dick Strong*

The magnificent ability of computers to organize data for us leads us to believe that there are certainties out there which, when found and properly put into a formula, will lead to continued success. I admit there seem to be specific market moves that lend themselves to certainties, usually after the fact. Then, when the certainty of one market time span is organized for the future, it normally does not work out that way. The market has a way of fooling all those who become sure of their own abilities.

*James L. Fraser*

The rate of return for a stock is inverse to the thickness of the research file.

*Michael Murphy*

You can never rest when you're running a growth fund.

*Dick Strong*

It is wise to remember that too much success in the stock market is itself an excellent warning.

*Gerald M. Loeb*

Over-thinking gets in the way of market success.

*David Upshaw*

I think it's a mistake to be dogmatic in this business. You have to function free of biases. Over the years, I've met so many people who are burdened with dogma. 'I will never buy a high-tech stock.' 'I'll never buy a stock that's near its high.' 'I'll never buy a stock that I used to own at a much lower price.' This game is rough enough without circumscribing one's activities with a lot of dogma.

*Peter B. Connell*

Wall Street has a way of killing a good thing by drowning it with excess funds.

*U.S. Trust Co.*

When there is a bull market fever in the air and everyone is talking about their winnings, there is intense pressure on the investor to participate. This pressure may have a tendency to cloud judgment and cause one to reach for stocks he would ordinarily avoid.

*Peter B. Connell*

The thing that separates the men from boys in this industry is the willingness to buy stocks when they are down.

*James Barrow*

The initial sickening slide in a bear market is then followed by a bear-market or sucker's rally. Then equities get slammed again, to be followed yet again by a sucker's rally. The process repeats itself until just about everyone throws up their hands in utter despair, convinced that the market will never again sustain a big move higher. 'Just let me get even, and then I will never go near stocks again!' is the cry from many. That's the bottom.

*Steve Forbes*

When a market trend goes for twenty years, it appears normal.

*Charlie Mehar*

Popularity is a great thing in our personal lives but a dangerous thing in the stock market.

*Al Goldman*

If you wait for someone to ring a bell or blow a whistle before you invest, it's too late.

*Monte Gordon*

It takes conviction to stand firm, of course, and not everyone can do it. Some people bend under the onslaught of negative news and views. Others are compelled to sell because they need the money. But those who can hold out during negative times are likely to be as well rewarded in the future as they have been in the past. Maybe even more so.

*Sir John Templeton*

My suggestion is to pay less attention to short-term market forecasts and to concentrate on longer-term themes and expected changes in the investment and economic climates. The experts should offer some good clues, but successful investing requires both patience and the perception of changes in long-term themes.

*Robert Farrell*

Any clear consensus, whether it's bullish or bearish, whether it's from lay people or experts, has to be at least questioned, because, by the time something becomes obvious to the majority of us, it rarely has much profit left in it. The market is a discounting mechanism.

*Robert Farrell*

October is one of the particularly dangerous months to speculate in stocks. Others are November, December, January, February, March, April, May, June, July, August, and September.

*Mark Twain*

Day to day market is fashion, but over a period of time it is owning a business.

*Roger Lipton*

Why do stocks typically outperform bonds? A major reason is that businesses retain earnings, with these going on to generate still more earnings—and dividends, too.

*Warren Buffett*

What should investors do? In the last 70 years, if you were willing to buy into declines, you were always rewarded. I always bought into declines even though my fund always fell during those declines. Once you've decided what money you want to risk over the next three to five years, choose good, sound companies; then rely on your faith in the companies. One other point: You must keep in mind that there's always something to worry about. In the 1950s and 1960s, we were consumed by fear of nuclear war. Houses were being built with fallout shelters, and the market tripled in the '50s and doubled in the '60s.

*Peter Lynch*

Going short is betting on something that'll happen. If you go short for meaningful amounts, you can go broke. If something is selling for twice what it is worth, what's to stop it from selling for ten times what it is worth? You'll be right eventually, but you may be explaining it to somebody in the poorhouse.

*Warren Buffett (1993)*

By the time the Fed is ready to slow things down and raise interest rates, greed has taken over. Investors are full of themselves and they ignore the Fed signals.

*Dick Strong*

Those who flee stock mutual funds when prices are depressed, as so many shareholders did just before the latest run-up, are their own worst enemies.

*Louis Rukeyser*

What you learn on the news today has almost nothing to do with what the market does tomorrow.

*Carlton G. Lutts*

**Horse Sense. Street Smarts.**

Buying stocks just for the purpose of being fully invested is idiotic.

*Jean-Marie Eveillard*

Bull markets begin at the point of maximum pessimism. Bear markets begin at the point of maximum optimism.

*Sir John Templeton*

If you are oriented toward absolute returns, you can't be confined to a narrow field of investments.

*Jean-Marie Eveillard*

There is no such thing as a disaster proof portfolio.

*Warren Buffett*

Patience rewards investors more when the trend is up than when the trend is down.

*Don Hodges*

Our biggest mistakes have been made by expanding in good markets, not in bad ones. Opportunities to build your base are better during difficult times.

*Craig Hall, Hall Financial Group*

A bull market is like a relay-race in which dynamic, growing sectors pass the baton.

*David Saito-Chung*

"Neither life nor the stock market is that predictable. I wish it were that simple, and then we would all be rich.

*Al Goldman*

Individual stocks can rise or fall 50% for no good reason.

*Benjamin Graham*

We must know ourselves better than our stocks; we must deal with our own rationality more than with our stocks' ratios; we must cope with our transient irrationality more than with the fugitive fluctuations of our portfolios.

*Al Frank*

Market tops and bottoms are made by emotion, not facts.

*Jim Weiss*

The only thing we have to fear is the absence of fear itself. When investors are fearless and complacency reigns in the market—the 20's and the 90's—stocks almost always are poised to fall.

*Erin E. Arvedlund*

Out of the market? Never! Investors who sit on cash never make any money.

*Phil Carret*

Remember the price you pay will determine your profit when you sell.

*Ralph Coleman*

Every time you think you've found the key to the market, some S.O.B. changes the lock.

*Gerald M. Loeb*

The market: in the short run, it's a voting machine; in the long run, it's a weighing machine.

*Warren Buffett*

The markets behave in ways, sometimes for a very long stretch, that are not linked to value. Sooner or later, value counts.

*Warren Buffett*

You can't make back in the alley what you lost on Main Street.

*Harold Watkins*

We have most of our success buying overlooked, boring stocks.

*Ann Miletti*

If you expect to continue to purchase stock throughout your life, you should welcome price declines as a way to add stocks more cheaply to your portfolio.

*Warren Buffett*

There is no evidence that profitable market timing can be done on a consistent basis. But there is sufficient evidence to suggest that market timing involves extreme risk of being out of the market at the wrong time.

*Bob Anslow*

Unless you can watch your stock holdings decline by 50% without becoming panic-stricken, you should not be in the stock market.

*Warren Buffett*

When you hear someone talking about 'guidance' on Wall Street, just remember who's really doing the steering—the captain who's trying to take you for a ride on his boat.

*Christopher Byron*

An investment operation is one which, upon thorough analysis, promises safety of principal and a satisfactory return. Operations not meeting these requirements are speculative. The value of analysis diminishes as the element of chance increases.

*Graham & Dodd Security Analysis 1934*

Don't sell something because you're despondent. Look at a company's valuation, not what price you paid for it. The fact that you could be down 50, 60, 70% on something is totally irrelevant. If you think the company is a compelling value at the current price, then it's something you should hold or add to.

*Richie Freeman*

Investing is not a game of perfect.

*Don Hays*

A key to investing is that you can't be afraid to make mistakes.

*George Vanderheiden*

Most people do not have a long-term horizon when the market goes down.

*Richard Fisher*

There's no question that patient, long-term investing is the surest way to wealth for most people.

*Louis Rukeyser*

Write it down. Engrave it in stone or at least into the wall. Surrounding conditions always look great at market tops.

*Sy Harding*

Market research tells you what happened yesterday. Sensitivity tells you where the world is going.

*Ronald Shaich*

We do not want to maximize the price at which Berkshires trades. We wish for them to trade in a narrow range centered at intrinsic business value.

*Warren Buffett*

An overvalued stock can be as damaging to the long-run health of a company as an undervalued stock.

*Joseph Fuller, Michael C. Jensen*

The more difficult it is to take action in the market, the more likely it is to be successful.

*Dick Davis*

You make most of your money in bear markets. You just don't realize it at the time.

*S. R. Davis*

Investment focus should be on value not on trends.

*Sir John Templeton*

All of the great advances and declines of the past twenty years have been surprises to me.

*Peter Lynch*

In the old days when we had shorter cycles, I'd shock people by selling things; well...I'd sell because there was no reason to sell. If there's a reason to sell, the stock's not going to be there (high). If you just sell into strength, you are going to end up winning if you just have the patience...

*Bill Sams*

Nobody can predict interest rates, the future direction of the economy or the stock market. Dismiss all such forecasts and concentrate on what's actually happening to the companies in which you've invested.

*Peter Lynch*

We all know that money placed at the bottom of a decline can be multiplied many times over in any succeeding bull market. So we try to figure out when that bottom is on hand and yet we are usually frozen to the handle of the money pump until the investment climate looks rewarding. When it looks rewarding, stock prices are significantly higher or the climate would not be looking so good.

*James L. Fraser*

Once it becomes evident that a stock won't meet my expectations, I have no trouble selling, 'no matter what.' Also, if I set parameters on buying stocks, my record would be no better than anyone else's. There is no simple formula. It's hard to generalize about so many different companies in so many circumstances.

*Ken Heebner*

Buy when most people—including experts—are pessimistic, and sell when they actively optimistic.

*Benjamin Graham*

The most common cause of low prices for stocks is pessimism— sometimes pervasive, and sometimes specific to a company or an industry. We want to do business in such an environment, not because we like pessimism, but because we like the prices it produces. It's optimism that's the enemy of the rational buyer. None of this means, however, that a business or a stock is an intelligent purchase simply because it is unpopular. A strict contrarian approach is just as foolish as a follow-the-crowd strategy. One piece of advice that I got at Columbia University from Ben Graham that I've never forgotten: 'You're neither right nor wrong because other people agree with you. You're right because your facts are right and your reasoning is right. That's the only thing that makes you right.'

*Warren Buffett*

Markets go up in anticipation of good news. The beginning of such anticipation, and not the good news itself, is the beginning of a bull market.

*Sir John Templeton*

You might consider bear markets not to be a catastrophe, a reason to sell or to drop out of the market, but as an opportunity, a chance to buy at a relatively low price.

*Sir John Templeton*

Patience is often worth more than money in this business

*Charles Almon*

Our permanent holdings have three things in common. First, they have good fundamental economic characteristics. Second, they have management that is very able and very trustworthy. Third, we like the companies. We like what they do, find them interesting, and like being associated with them. We look for businesses that we can understand. We don't want to stray from that.

*Warren Buffett*

It is not prudent to sacrifice principle for the sake of yield.

*Anonymous*

Successful investing is like watching a magician, if you look where the action is, you'll be misled.

*Geraldine Weiss*

Time is the friend of the wonderful business, the enemy of the mediocre...it is far better to buy a wonderful company at a fair price than a fair company at a wonderful price.

*Warren Buffett*

Our criteria have nothing to do with maximizing immediately reportable earnings. Our goal, rather, is to maximize eventual net worth

*Warren Buffett*

Don't avoid risk; assess risk.

*Don Hodges*

The faster a stock price moves around, the greater the chance that you will buy or sell at the wrong time:

*Kevin B. Waide*

I have never accumulated a major position in a stock that did not go down after I first bought it.

*Laurence Tisch*

We all know that stock prices ebb and flow in accordance with the opinions of buyers and sellers. We have learned that stock prices are human conclusions as to values. There are trends of thought in the stock market, exactly as there are in art, literature, and science.

These trends of opinion concerning stock values become, in turn, the trends of stock prices.

*Humphrey Neill*

The short term, the next month or year, depends very heavily on human emotions. The long term, however, depends on values—and values keep rising.

*Sir John Templeton*

Bad markets are always followed by good markets.

*Dick Davis*

If everybody owns it, it will go down. If nobody owns it, it may go up.

*James Barrow*

Selling is the most difficult part of investing.

*Bill Nasgovitz*

I cannot understand why an investor of that sort elects to put money into a business that is his 20th favorite rather than simply adding money to his top choices—the businesses he understands the best and that present the least risk along with the greatest profit potential. In the words of the prophet Mae West; 'Too much of a good thing can be wonderful.'

*Warren Buffett*

We decided long ago that in an investment lifetime, it's just too hard to make hundreds of smart decisions. Therefore, we adopted a strategy that required our being smart—and not too smart at that—only a very few times. Indeed, we'll now settle for one good idea a year.

*Warren Buffett*

The biggest mistakes I have made in the stock market are with companies with a lot of promise, but no earnings.

*Peter Lynch*

To be sure, the foundation under a contrarian investor is that the majority is usually wrong in the stock market. It seems simple to say that you should buy low and sell high, though one never knows what is the lowest price or the highest price until after the fact. What we mean to do, as investors, are to accumulate when stocks are low and sell when they are high. As we do this, it is seldom clear that we are doing the right thing unless we work within a contrary opinion thinking framework.

*James L. Fraser*

The four most costly words in investing: this time it's different.

*Walter Deemer*

Once you've made up your mind to buy or sell a security, wait two days. You will usually get a better price.

*W. J. Gault*

We have been investment counselors for 58 years, and in all that time, we have never been able to tell our clients when a bear market will start or stop.

*Sir John Templeton*

It takes conviction to stand firm, of course, and not everyone can do it. Some people bend under the onslaught of negative news, and views. Others are compelled to sell because they need the money.

*Sir John Templeton*

If we can assume that it is the habit of the market to overvalue common stocks which have been showing excellent growth or are glamorous for some other reason, it is logical to expect that it will undervalue—relatively at least—companies that are out of favor because of unsatisfactory developments of a temporary nature. This may be set down as a fundamental law of the stock market, and it suggests an investment approach that should prove most conservative and promising.

*Benjamin Graham*

The market, in its own diabolical fashion, likes to do all it can to separate the investor from his money. The greener the investor, the more easily the market succeeds. At market tops, for instance, it will bask in good news, drawing in the last dime from widows and orphans. As market bottoms approach, it will cry out with a hundred terrible news items, convincing all but the most stalwart investors that the world is going to pot and that they should sell before their accounts dwindle to nothingness.

*Carlton Lutts*

The doomsayers work by extrapolation; they take a trend and extend it, forgetting that the doom factor sooner or later generates a coping mechanism. You cannot extrapolate any series in which the human element intrudes.

*Barton Biggs*

Remember stocks are never low unless there are great disturbances in financial markets, business, or the global arena. The more complex and inter-related the disturbances, the more investors tend to sell. The selling usually is done through worry or fear of pending developments, though some is done through financial necessity because of over-leveraging. Our instinct of fear allows us to act in sympathy with the crowd. Low prices result, without conscious reason, then one does not buy stocks again until they are higher, when the sky is blue.

*James l. Fraser*

Growth drives stocks up while strong balance sheets keep them from going down.

*David Ellison*

''We not only have statistical evidence that the majority have always been led by human impulses to make wrong moves, and to lose money, but it is a simple process of reasoning to prove that the majority of us must always be wrong in the market and are certain to lose. To begin with, we know that to gain profit, one must buy when prices are comparatively low and sell when prices are higher, but if most

**Horse Sense. Street Smarts.**

people had the foresight to take advantage of low prices and buy, then the low prices wouldn't exist, since there would then be more buyers than sellers. Likewise, if the majority of us were cagey enough to sell the instant that stocks are priced beyond their worth, then peak prices would never be reached.

*Fred C. Kelly*

On Leverage: Our consistently conservative financial policies may *appear* to have been a mistake, but in my view were not. We might have seen only a 1% chance that some shock factor would cause a conventional debt ratio to produce a result falling somewhere between temporary anguish and default. We wouldn't like those odds. A small chance of distress or disgrace cannot, in our view, be offset by a large chance of extra returns. If your actions are sensible, you are certain to get good results; in most cases, leverage just moves things along faster. Charlie and I have never been in a big hurry, we enjoy the process more than the proceeds—though we have learned to live with those also.

*Warren Buffett*

The areas of the market that hold up relatively well in a bear market are telegraphing the fact that they are going to be leaders of the next bull market.

*Walter Deemer*

Despite the capital market convulsions, wars, stock market bubbles and crashes, it turns out that stocks still track profits in the long run. From time to time stocks get ahead of profits, or fall behind. But over the long run, the two will grow together.

*John Dessauer*

Survival is the only road to riches. You should try to maximize return only if losses would not threaten your survival and if you have a compelling future need for the extra gains you might earn.

*Peter Bernstein*

I have always thought that if, even in the very presence of dizzily rising prices, we had all continuously repeated, 'two and two make four', much of the evil might have been averted. Similarly, even in the general moment of gloom, when many begin to wonder if declines will ever halt, the appropriate abracadabra may be They always did.

*Bernard Baruch*

There are a few things that I really think are worth knowing about:

1. The principle of regression to the mean

2. Long base breakouts

3. Exponential blow-off patterns

4. Hope, fear, and greed rule the markets.

The bells and whistles change from cycle to cycle. The ticker symbols of the hot stocks change. But the game is changeless. We tend to be greedy at tops and fearful at bottoms. History may not repeat exactly, but it rhymes.

*David Upshaw*

Find a mentor—someone who has had success making people money over several years and cycles, and work under that mentor to learn the business. Get as much financial education as possible.

*Craig Hodges*

When you buy bad companies, they are always worse than you thought.

*Anders Scharp*

If management isn't willing to invest its funds in its own company's future, why should you? Give me the company whose management covets its shares, clings to them through generations, and shares a common interest with its shareholders simply because they are one and the same. These managements are rewarded or penalized simultaneously with their shareholders. No conflicts of interest here.

*Elliott Schlang*

**Horse Sense. Street Smarts.**

The worst companies sell at the best multiples and the best at the worst multiples.

*Julian Robertson*

People entering the financial business should be given a ticket with 20 numbers on it. Each time a stock is bought, a hole should be punched in the ticket. After all 20 numbers have been punched; no further purchases should be made in a person's lifetime.

*Warren Buffett*

Our problem is that the herd is still there under waves of pluralism and adversity. We all want to do the same thing at times, and usually in markets, we lose when we do.

*James L. Fraser*

Good times or bad, markets are the place to look for clues to the future.

*Robert M. Bleiberg*

If you search worldwide, you will find more bargains and better bargains than by studying only one nation. You will also gain the advantage of diversification.

*Sir John Templeton*

Learn to control your emotions of fear and greed, and have the patience to not expect instant gratification.

*Bill Berger*

We try to buy companies that we don't have to sell.

*Bill Berger*

To avoid having all your eggs in the wrong basket at the wrong time, diversify.

*Sir John Templeton*

There are no growth companies; there are only companies that are in the growth period.

*Bill Berger*

The more exciting the company, the more money you are about to lose.

*Alex Paris*

In economics, interest rates act as gravity behaves in the physical world. At all times, in all markets, in all parts of the world, the tiniest change in rates changes the value of every financial asset. You see that clearly with the fluctuating prices of bonds. But the rule applies as well to farmland, oil reserves, stocks, and every other financial asset. And the effects can be huge on values. If interest rates are, say 13%, the present value of a dollar that you're going to receive in the future from an investment is not nearly as high as the present value of a dollar if rates are 4%.

*Warren Buffett*

But those who can hold out during negative times are likely to be as well rewarded in the future as they have been in the past.

*Sir John Templeton*

We must know ourselves better than our stocks; we must deal with our own rationality more than with our stocks rations; we must cope with our transient irrationality more than with the fugitive fluctuations of our portfolios.

*Al Frank*

Investment success is achieved by coupling good business judgment with an ability to insulate one's thoughts and behavior from the super-contagious emotions that are currently swirling in the marketplace.

*Doug Kass*

All we have to do is get it right 60% of the time and we are doing great. We can afford to make four mistakes in ten and still beat the

market. We look at the down-side first; most people look at the up-side first.

George Vanderheiden

After spending many years in Wall Street, and after making and losing millions of dollars, I want to tell you this. It was never my thinking that made the big money for me. It was my sitting. My sitting tight. Men who can be both right and sit tight are uncommon. I found it one of the hardest things to learn. But it is only after a stock operator has firmly grappled with this that he can make his money.

Edwin LeFevre, Jesse Livermore

Investment success is achieved by coupling good business judgment with an ability to insulate one's thoughts and behavior from the super-contagious emotions that are currently swirling in the marketplace.

Doug Kass

Since 1920, the market has had forty declines of 10% or more. To be a successful investor, you must understand that it is perfectly natural and provides portfolio managers and investors alike with an investment opportunity. Investors, who fail to recognize this, and instead rely on a short-term outlook, are nearly always disappointed.

Peter Lynch

Be an owner—don't try to time. Just as you buy a house for a generation, own equities or funds for a generation. In 25 years, a lot of near term will look silly.

Shelby Davis

When you hear that a stock is going to be 'the next', just block it out. The next Toys R Us didn't work, the next Home Depot didn't work, and the next Xerox didn't work. Anytime you hear 'the next anything', just forget it.

Peter Lynch

Things are never as good as they seem. They are never as bad as they seem. It is understanding that basic principle that allows you to invest money at times when other people are running.

*Chuck Royce*

Real Investment Opportunities do not come dressed in Sunday clothes or with brass bands playing. Rather, at first glance, they appear to be dubious. Interesting, perhaps, but uncertain. And this is exactly why they are opportunities for the great mass of the general public, and their advisors have not yet discovered them.

Their prices have not yet been discounted to the point of absurdity. Their virtues have not yet been exaggerated, to the point of ridiculousness. Consequently they present opportunities for really substantial price appreciation and profit.

*Nathan Rothschild*

Don't worry about predicting the stock market or economy. Trying to predict the market is a total waste of time.

*Peter Lynch*

Buy'em when told by others to defer.

*James L. Fraser*

If you buy stocks cheaply enough, you don't have to watch them.

*Phil Carret*

Buy a company when its stock price is 50% below the company's per share underlying value. Sell any asset when you have found another asset which is a 50% better buy.

*Sir John Templeton*

The market has a tendency to do that which most of us think it won't do. It loves to humiliate us.

*James A. Shambo*

There's that company that has all the right elements and makes you so excited that you'd be willing to take out a loan at 10% to buy stock in it, or even go to work for them yourself. That's when you know you have a winner.

The most important quality for an investor is temperament, not intellect. You don't need tons of IQ in this business. You don't have to be able to play three dimensional chess or duplicate bridge. You need a temperament that neither derives great pleasure from being with the crowd or against the crowd. You know you're right, not because of the position of others, but because your facts and your reasoning are right. Most investors do not really think of themselves as owning a piece of the business.

The real test of whether you are investing from a value standpoint or not is whether you care if the stock market opens tomorrow. If you've made a good investment, it shouldn't bother you if they close down the stock market for five years. You own a piece of a business at the right price and that's what's working for you. In 30 years of investing I have never bought a technology company. I don't understand any of them. So the technological revolution has gone right past me. I don't have to make money in every game.

There are all kinds of things I don't know about—like cocoa beans. But, so what! I don't have to know about everything. The securities business is the perfect business. Every day you literally have thousands of the major American corporations offered you at a price, and a price that changes daily and nothing is forced upon you. There are no called strikes in the business. The pitcher just stands there and throws balls at you and you can let as many go by as you want without a penalty. In real baseball, if the ball is between the knees and the shoulders you either swing or you get a strike called on you. If you get three strikes, you're called out.

In the securities business you stand there and they throw U.S. Steel at 28 and General Motors at 80, and you don't have to swing at any of them. They may be wonderful pitches, but if you don't know enough you don't have to swing. And you can stand there and watch thousands of pitches, and finally you get one right there where you

**The Stock Market**                                                          155

want it, something that you understand and is priced right, and then you swing.

*Warren Buffet*

Markets are never wrong; opinions are.

*Jesse Livermore*

Our business right now is being fueled by the rocket fuel of cheap debt. Rocket fuel is explosive and you have to be careful how you handle it.

*William E. Conway, Jr.*

What does it take to become a consistently successful money manager? Over time the most common answer is: a string of devastating losses. The investor who has lost heavily and stays in the game often becomes extremely successful later. Why? Because the losses first awaken powerful survival instincts, then allow the individual to develop a deep understanding of personal reactions to changes in the markets.

In time, the result is a potent intuition that can be informed and awakened more easily to our personal financial reward. The memory of past losses lurks in the background, continuing to stimulate the instincts which can guide us to financial security.

*Dessauer's Journal*

Performance is a lagging indicator of investment decision making. More often than not, when a money manager makes an exceptionally smart stock purchase, the wisdom of that move is not evident for several months or even a couple years. Multi-bagger stocks often look quite average, even mediocre, during the first year or two of ownership.

*Arne Alsin*

It's a given that the stock market knows everything you know plus ten thousand other facts and items. The stock market knows all about the housing mess, it knows about the US debts and deficits, it knows about the phony US/Chinese trade-off, it knows about the negative savings rate of US consumers, it knows about the high price of oil, it knows about Iran and its nuclear ambitions, it knows about the disaster of Iraq. It knows all that plus the other ten thousand facts and items—the market puts them all together and digests them.

*Richard Russell*

In an industry where new business models are emerging and change is so rapid, it's important for an analyst to monitor the broad secular trends that are taking shape.

*Brian Demain*

Technology is high risk; it's difficult to predict and highly volatile. You need to be very careful unless you understand it. Most investors don't.

*Stephen McClellan*

The trick comes from balancing risks and returns. You can't pick the bottom, and you certainly can't pick the top.

*David Decker*

Truly great athletes have short memories. They don't dwell on mistakes or revel in past successes. They focus on the matter at hand, drawing on their experience but keeping their focus squarely in the present. Similarly, the best investors don't beat themselves up over past mistakes. They don't obsess over the price they paid for a stock, and they never buy more of a stock merely to lower their average cost. They don't sell winners just to lock up a gain or hold losers to avoid booking a loss.

The best investors, in short, look forward. They learn from experience and strive for improvement, but they don't let the past keep them from doing what is right for the road ahead.

*Dow Theory Forecasts*

Quality of Earnings: The Investor's guide to how much a company is really making.

*Thornton Oglove*

If you're going to invest, you need to make a stand. And it isn't for the faint of heart. I don't care what stock you own, if you own it long enough, it will eventually go down more than 50%. But, psychologically, there is safety in numbers.

You will find to your astonishment stocks you never dreamed of will go up 10 to 20-fold. If you have a few of those, you can have 30 lemons out of 100 stocks. And don't try to rebalance your portfolio. You're always rebalancing automatically, when you own a lot of stocks.

*Thornton Oglove*

I've never made a dime predicting economic activity.

*Warren Buffett*

Risk management should be a process of dealing with the consequences of being wrong. Sometimes, these consequences are minimal. But betting the ranch on the assumption that prices can only go up should tell you the consequences would be more than minimal. Risk management should concentrate on limiting the size of the bet so you are not wiped out if you take the wrong side.

Risk management is fundamentally different from managing volatility. Volatility is often a symptom of risk but is not risk in and of itself. Volatility obscures the future but does not necessarily determine the future. Effective risk management starts with the recognition that any forecast can be wrong, and then weighs the consequences of being wrong.

*Peter Bernstein*

Beware of geeks bearing formulas.

*Warren Buffett*

When there is bull market fever in the air and everyone is talking about their winnings, there is intense pressure on the investor to participate. This pressure may have a tendency to cloud judgment and cause one to reach for stocks he would ordinarily avoid.

*Peter Connell*

In the manic phase, Mr. Market's enthusiasm puts a ridiculously high price on stocks. When he is depressed, Mr. Market's fears run away with him and he is so eager to sell stocks that his behavior is a little short of silly.

*Benjamin Graham*

The best time to invest is when you have money. This is because history suggests it is not timing the markets that matters. It is time.

*Sir John Templeton*

We are more than our investments. We are more than the year-to-year or day-by-day changes in our net worth. We are what we do for charity. We are how we treat our family and friends. We are how we treat our dogs and cats. We are what we do for our community and our nation. If you had $100 million or $100,000 a year ago and now you have a lot less, you are still the same person.

You are not a balance sheet, at least not one denominated in money, as was explained to me recently. Losing and making money are not moral issues so long as you are being honest. You may have a lot less money as this year ends than you did two years ago. But you are just as good or bad a person as you were then. It is a myth that money determines who you are, and if you have gotten over that myth by now, then 2008 will have been a very good year.

*Ben Stein*

A simple rule dictates my buying: Be fearful when others are greedy, and be greedy when others are fearful. And most certainly, fear is now widespread, gripping even seasoned investors. To be sure, investors are right to be wary of highly leveraged entities or businesses in weak competitive positions. But fears regarding the long-term prosperity of the nation's many sound companies make no sense.

These businesses will indeed suffer earnings hiccups, as they always have. But most major companies will be setting new profit records 5, 10, and 20 years from now. Let me be clear on one point: I can't predict the short-term movements of the stock market. I haven't the faintest idea as to whether stocks will be higher or lower a month— or a year—from now. What is likely, however, is that the market will move higher, perhaps substantially so, well before either sentiment or the economy turns up. So, if you wait for the robins, spring will be over.

*Warren Buffett*

Investing isn't just about probabilities. It's about consequences and you've got to be prepared for them.

*John Bogle*

The thing that separates the men from the boys in this industry is the willingness to buy stocks when they are down.

*James Barrow*

Since 1920, the market has had forty declines of 10% or more. To be a successful investor, you must understand that it is perfectly natural and provides portfolio managers and investors alike with an investment opportunity.

*Peter Lynch*

There's no such thing as a free lunch. And, certainly, nothing is good because you put a label on it, be it growth stocks or small cap stocks or hedge funds or private equity. And when people start saying that something is good because of what it is called, and then they are setting themselves to lose money. Chances are they will overpay and be disappointed.

*Howard Marks*

One part of the market is based on hard facts. One part is driven by human emotion. The short term, the next month or year depends

**Horse Sense. Street Smarts.**

very heavily on human emotions. Long term, however, depends on values and values keep rising.

*Sir John Templeton*

Mr. Madoff shifted investors' fears from risk that they might lose money to the risk they might lose out on making money.

*Jason Zweig*

The markets are random in the short term, cyclical in the medium term, and trending in the long term.

*Jim Otar*

Don't worry about predicting the stock market or economy. Trying to predict the market is a total waste of time.

*Peter Lynch*

The key to making money in stocks is not to get scared out of them.

*Peter Lynch*

Before this century is over, the Dow Jones Industrial Average will probably be over one million versus around 10,000 now. So for the long-term, the outlook is tremendously bullish if you buy stocks blindly to keep for a century.

*Sir John Templeton*

Most of the time common stocks are subject to irrational and excessive price fluctuations in both directions as the consequence of the ingrained tendency of most people to speculate or gamble...to give way to hope, fear and greed.

*Benjamin Graham*

Leverage giveth and Leverage taketh away.

*Norm Alster*

The real problem with models is that bankers tend to view them as 'cameras' that capture how the world works, like a camera that might photograph a physics experiment. Instead, they should be viewed as engines, since the presence of a model tends to change and drive market behavior in a way that makes it impossible to assume that the past can predict the future.

*Donald Mackenzie*

The future is never clear and you pay a high price for a cheery consensus. Uncertainty actually is the friend of the buyer of long term values.

*Warren Buffett*

The smart investors put their money into their retirement account and they don't chicken out just because the market drops in one year. The dumb ones buy when the market is up and they think it is going higher and they sell when the market is low and they think the market is going lower.

*Harry Markowitz*

Time after time I have been able to make a great buy because I knew something someone else didn't.

*Mark A. Roeder*

No market can fall everyday, just as no market can climb everyday. Indeed, some of the biggest one day surges in Wall Street history have occurred during bear markets.

*Jonah Keri*

Bull markets are born on pessimism grows on skepticism, mature on optimism, and die on euphoria.

*Sir John Templeton*

If you have a total intolerance for not making mistakes, you'll be unhappy in this business.

*Warren Buffett*

Because the stock market is forward-looking, it has little use for yesterday's or even today's crisis. The focus is always on the future—how will business be six months or a year or two from now.

*Norman Fosback*

There are just two basic questions that investors should care about: Is the management reasonably efficient and are the interests of the average outside shareholder receiving proper recognition.

*Benjamin Graham*

Everything will be all right. We do have the greatest economic machine that man has ever created, I believe. We started with four million people back in 1790 and look where we've come, and it wasn't because we were smarter than other people, it wasn't because our land was more fertile or we had more minerals or our climate was more favorable. We had a system that worked. It unleashed the human potential. Didn't work every year, we had six panics in the 19th century; in the 20th century, we had the Great Depression and World Wars, all kinds of things.

But we have a system, largely free market, rule of law, equality of opportunity, all of those things that cause the potential of humans to get unleashed, and we're far from done. So, I think your kids will live better than mine; your grandchildren will live better than your kids. There's no question about that. But the machine gets gummed up from time to time, and if you take the bulk of those centuries, probably 15 years were bad years, but we go forward.

*Warren Buffett*

Basically, price fluctuations have only one significant meaning for the true investor. They provide him with an opportunity to buy wisely when prices fall sharply and to sell wisely when they advance a great deal. At other times he will do better if he forgets about the stock market and pays attention to the dividend returns and to the operating results of his companies.

*Whitney Tilson*

Bull markets are born in despair when most investors have given up hope of stocks ever rising again.

*Neil Donahoe*

In many cases, stocks that advance dramatically by 20% or more in one to four weeks are the most powerful stocks of all—capable of doubling, tripling or more.

*William J. O'Neil*

The first two years of a new bull market typically provide your best and safest period, but they require courage, patience, and profitable sitting.

*William J. O'Neil*

It's always easier to explain the market's move than to predict them.

*James Stewart*

Leaders in strong markets fall 72% in subsequent bear markets.

*William O'Neil*

Stocks are like people, they never look so good as they do at their peak.

*Donald H. Gold*

When you buy a stock, forget what you paid for it.

*Truman Smith*

Cost basis should not be considered when you are thinking of selling a company.

*Warren Buffett*

When looking at buying a company, focus on what the business is worth, not the stock price.

*Warren Buffett*

The markets are like a pendulum.

*Lindsay Davis*

There are, in reality, only two kinds of people in Wall Street: those who have made very serious errors in their short-term judgments—and the liars.

*Louis Rukeyser*

The way to lose money in mutual funds is simple: buy them when stocks are hurtling into the stratosphere, then sell them the first time the market trips and tumbles.

*Louis Rukeyser*

It's unwise to base investing decisions on what's worked well in the markets in recent months or even the last one, three, and five years.

*Stephen P. Utkus*

Basing your investment on the profit and loss statement rather than the balance sheet is an absurd way to analyze securities.

*John Bogle*

We have short memories on screwing up. There's no shame. Just start over and do it again. This pessimism will fade. The jobs will follow and we'll move on. That's my take on the United States.

*Shad Rowe*

Fortunately, in the stock market, there are no 4th quarters, no final stretch, no final bells, no final round, no last play. There is always a new day, a new beginning, a new season, a potential change in direction.

*Don Hodges*

The point of research is to cut through emotion and to bring a more rational perspective. Research permits you to do the unpopular, and the unpopular is almost always the most profitable.

*Lew Sanders*

If what everybody knows comes true the stock price won't change. Therefore, the best company in the world is not a good investment if everybody thinks it's the best company in the world.

*Eric J. Marshall*

While individual stocks may be pulled along momentarily by a strong bull market, ultimately, it is the individual stocks that determine the market, not vice versa.

*Sir John Templeton*

Often the best investments for the future are those that have been performing the worst.

*Stephen P. Utkus*

Remember, in most instances, you are buying either earnings or assets.

*Sir John Templeton*

The only way to avoid mistakes is not to invest—which is the biggest mistake of all. So, forgive yourself for your errors. Don't become discouraged and certainly don't try to recoup your losses by taking risks. Instead, turn each mistake into a learning experience.

*Sir John Templeton*

What always impresses me is how much the relaxed, long-term owners of stock do with their portfolios than the traders do with their portfolios with their switching of inventory. The relaxed investor is usually better informed and more understanding of essential value; he is more patient and less emotional; he pays smaller capital gain taxes; he does not incur unnecessary brokerage commissions; he avoids behaving like Cassius by 'thinking too much'.

*Lucien Hooper*

The stock market and the economy do not always march in lockstep. Bear markets do not always coincide with recessions and an overall decline in corporate earnings does not always cause a simultaneous decline in stock prices. So, buy individual stocks, not the market trend or economic outlook.

*Sir John Templeton*

No bull market is permanent. No bear market is permanent. There are no stocks that you can buy and forget. Remember, no investment is forever.

*Sir John Templeton*

Financial advisors have no more insight into whether the market is going to go up or down than anyone else.

*Thomas Murphy*

Everything is in a constant state of change, and the wise investor recognizes that success is a process of continually seeking answers to new generations.

*Sir John Templeton*

Most successful investors don't concern themselves with movements in the broad economy but instead focus on what they can control: building a sensible asset allocation, keeping expenses low, saving enough and not panicking amid market turmoil.

*Christine Benz*

Good investing is where you have the luxury of not having to participate in the market at all times. You can pick and choose the most appropriate time where the odds and probabilities of success are highly in your favor.

*Robert Fetch*

The last time I made any stock market predictions was in the year 1914, when my firm judged me qualified to write their daily market letter, based on the fact that I had one month's experience in Wall Street. Since then I have given up making predictions.

*Benjamin Graham*

Don't anticipate market moves with your hard-earned cash...the successful speculator must abandon his predictions, and follow the action of the market.

*Jesse Livermore*

The key to staying on top of the stock market is not predicting or knowing what the market is going to do. It's knowing and understanding what the market has actually done in the past several weeks and what it is currently doing now.

*William J. O'Neil*

We've long felt that the only value of stock forecasters is to make fortune tellers look good.

*Warren Buffett*

I don't read, much less follow, the valuations or predictions. I study the numbers.

*John Neff*

If you believe you or anyone else has a system that can predict the future of the stock market, the joke is on you.

*Ralph Wanger*

Time is much more important than timing when it comes to long-term market success.

*Dow Theory Forecasts*

The action of the market itself can be expected under most circumstances to stimulate buying or selling in a manner consistent enough to allow reasonably accurate forecasting of news in advance of its actual occurrence.

*Gerald Loeb*

Volatility is more a measure of opportunity than risk. It lets me act on the visceral reactions of others. Value is the result of panic selling – irrational, illogical selling. To be good at what we do, we have to be strong financial analysts, strong business analysts, and pretty good psychologists. Our goal, over the long term, is to provide equity-like returns with less risk than the market. We want to make sure the odds and potential payoff are in our favor. If all we can make is 20 percent, but we could also lose 20 percent, then it's not that appealing. If we think we could make 60 percent vs. maybe losing 20 percent, that may be worth the risk.

*Steven Romick*

The market is always making mountains out of molehills and exaggerating ordinary vicissitudes into major setbacks.

*Benjamin Graham*

Don't take forecasts too seriously and don't view them as the literal truth. Few people get forecasts right very often.

*Byron R. Wien*

Many individuals sell stocks that perform well to take their profits. Meanwhile, they hold onto those that perform poorly, hoping for a recovery. In other words, they cut their flowers and water their weeds. Follow that strategy for very long and you'll eventually have a portfolio of under-performing investments.

*Edward Jones strategist*

Often there is no correlation between the success of a company's operations and the success of its stock over a few months or even a few years. In the long term, there is 100% correlation in the success of the company and the success of its stock.

*Peter Lynch*

Under financial pressure, most people do not and cannot think dispassionately until it's too late. They choke because they wait too long to sell thinking their situation will improve.

*Paul Sullivan*

Sell losers and ride winners.

*Ace Greenberg*

It is absurd to think that the general public can ever make money out of market forecasts.

*Benjamin Graham*

If a prediction says stocks will go up, and everyone believes it, the crowd is then likely to drive up prices very rapidly – until it is convinced that prices are too high and begins to drive them back down.

*Jeff Sommer*

About the only thing guaranteed when it comes to equities is that the market will go through alternating bouts of depression and euphoria.

*Al Frank*

Far more money has been lost in anticipation of a correction than has been lost in the corrections themselves.

*Peter Lynch*

The market is better at predicting the news than the news is at predicting the market.

*Gerald Loeb*

When extraordinary high returns are promised in a supposedly low-risk investment, that's a tell-tale sign that something likely is amiss.

*Stephen L. Cohen*

Most investors are not good when they get in the market or when they get out.

*Laurence Fink*

The stock market will come and go, but friends and family will be there forever.

*Cade Culver*

It's going to be ugly, but that's when it's time to buy. I'm going to buy and get crushed, and then I'm going to make a lot of money.

Barron's Online

# Work Ethic

**Tim Cox,** *Western Skies*

The whole structure of society is based on the fact that people HAVE to work. That is not entirely true. Depending on how you define the term, work can be rewarding, or it can be drudgery. A person should find out as early as possible what their lifework or calling is going to be.

Finding that calling determines, more than likely, how satisfying and rewarding your work—and thus, your life—can be. Your work can be a delightful part of your self-identity. It can bring you great pleasure and provide a valuable service to others. As they say, any job worth doing is worth doing well. Find the worth in your job. Turn your work into joy.

Don't ever sit and watch someone else work. Get up and help.

*William Brown*

I've never seen luck jump on a guy sitting in the shade.

*Darrell Royal*

Be willing to make decisions. That's the most important quality in a good leader. Don't fall victim to what I call the "ready-aim-aim-aim" syndrome. You must be willing to fire.

*Boone Pickens*

If you do just a little more that your competitors, you'll stand head and shoulders above them.

*Ed Moore*

What gets measured gets done.

*Peter Drucker*

The work we are now doing is, I trust, done for posterity, in such a way they need not repeat it. We shall delineate with correctness the great arteries of this country; those who come after us will fill up the canvas we begin.

*Thomas Jefferson*

I certainly don't believe in winning at all costs, if that means cheating or doing things that are wrong.

*Tom Landry*

To strive, to find, and not to yield.

*Erik Jonsson*

Only capitalists can destroy capitalism. Populist capitalism of a type is very beneficial to the vast majority in our system, but an ethical tradition is needed to make it all work. When you have senior people walking away with hundreds of millions, leaving everyone else in the dirt, that is hugely depressing and very dangerous.

*Felix G. Rohatyn*

**Horse Sense. Street Smarts.**

There are two kinds of career paths. There is the one that takes you straight to the top very quickly, but burns you out very fast. There is another way in which you grow and study and become better and better. That way, your career rises steadily and allows you to achieve some longevity.

*Nat King Cole*

A wise man fights to win, but he is twice a fool who has no plan for possible defeat.

*Louis L'Amour*

If I had eight hours to chop down a tree, I'd spend six hours sharpening my ax.

*Abraham Lincoln*

A man should keep on being constructive and do constructive things until it's time to die. He should live life and make every day count, to the very end.

*John Willard Marriott*

What the wise man does at the beginning, the fool does at the end.

*Warren Buffet*

Far too many executives have become more concerned with the "four P's"—pay, perks, power and prestige—rather than making profits for shareholders.

*Boone Pickens*

Never let the prospect of a paycheck get in the way of telling the truth. Always put clients' interests first, and only take on work where you can provide true value.

*Marvin Bower*

You must feel that you have a project every day when you get up, even if it goes nowhere. You've got to challenge yourself everyday.

*Norman Lloyd*

He is a wise man who wastes no energy on pursuits for which he is not fitted; and he is wiser still who from among the things he can do well, chooses and resolutely follows the best.

*William Gladstone*

We must take care to launch ourselves with as strong and decided an initiative as possible.

*William James*

To win at golf, one must practice religiously—there IS no substitute.

*Doug Sanders*

Work brings profit; talk brings poverty.

*Proverbs 14:23*

A little neglect may breed great mischief...for want of a nail the shoe was lost; for want of a shoe the horse was lost; and for want of a horse the rider was lost.

*Anonymous*

Courage is the main quality of leadership: courage to initiate something and keep it going, a pioneering spirit, an adventurous spirit, the courage to blaze new trails in our land of opportunity.

*Walt Disney*

Steady plodding brings prosperity—hasty speculation brings poverty.

*Proverbs 21:5*

Wealth from gambling quickly disappears; wealth from hard work grows.

*Proverbs 13: 11*

Seize the very first opportunity to act on every resolution you make, and on every emotional prompting you may experience in the direction of the habits you aspire to gain.

*William James*

**Horse Sense. Street Smarts.**

If you think you are beaten, you are. If you think that you dare not, you don't. If you'd like to win, but you think you can't, it's almost certain you won't.

*Anonymous*

If we believe in what we do, we will do it better.

*Petronius, 63 A.D.*

I'm not as smart as most people I've run across in my travels. While I couldn't outsmart anybody, there was one thing I could do. I could work harder and longer than anybody else was willing to work.

*Bill Veeck*

## Workmanship

Your true value to society comes when someone says, "Let me see your work. A glib tongue may open a door or two, and artful use of the right fork may win an approving nod. But, the real test of one's worth can be measured by the care given to the job at hand: a budget to plan, a solo to play, a report to draft, a leaky sink that needs fixing. The next time you write a memo, make sure you get all of the facts straight. Pay attention to those details. Don't sweat the small Stuff.

*United Technologies Ad*

Plans are only good intentions unless they immediately degenerate into hard work.

*Peter Drucker*

Play every game for all your worth, but when it's over it's over.

*T. G. Hall*

A goal not written down is only a wish.

*Emmitt Smith, III*

Never stifle a thought to take action. Do it. You'll be richly rewarded.

*Don Hodges*

Before it is possible to achieve anything, an objective must be set. Many people flounder about in life because they do not have a purpose, an objective toward which to work. Setting that objective is only one step. The other essential is to become determined to achieve it.

*George Halas*

Work hard. Come early, stay late. That's the way leadership has to approach it.

*Boone Pickens*

I see what keeps people young: work.

*Ted Turner*

There is no short cut to success. It takes practice.

*Otto Graham*

You can do anything if you have enthusiasm. Enthusiasm is the yeast that makes your hopes rise to the stars. Enthusiasm is the sparkle in your eyes, the swing in your gait, the grip of your hand, the irresistible surge of will and energy to execute your ideas. Enthusiasts are fighters. They have fortitude. They have staying qualities. Enthusiasm is at the bottom of all progress. With it, there is accomplishment. Without it, there are only alibis.

*Henry Ford*

I choose to believe that whenever I was doing nothing, someone else was catching up and taking everything I had. I've never been better at anything than anybody else, which meant that I always would have to work a little harder to keep up or maybe even pull ahead. Like the turtle who raced the hare, I plowed forward, slow and steady.

*Jay Leno*

You can't build a reputation on what you are going to do.

*Henry Ford*

**Horse Sense. Street Smarts.**

What we become depends on what we read after all the professors are finished with us. The greatest university of all is the collection of books.

*Thomas Carlyle*

Whatever you do, try to take it to the level of an art.

*Bill Russell*

You have to do what you have to do, to do what you want to do.

*Kurt Wulf*

To make a difference in the real world is to put ten times as much into everything as anyone thinks is reasonable.

*Daniel Vasella*

Wealth depends chiefly on two words, industry and frugality: that is, waste neither time nor money, but make the best of both.

*Benjamin Franklin*

Players should keep poise on the field and not panic, especially when the pressure is at its worst, and should always execute assignments flawlessly, without making mistakes. You cannot win unless you execute properly and you cannot execute unless you maintain your poise.

*Weeb Ewbank*

I am always doing things I can't do. That's how I get to do them.

*Pablo Picasso*

I didn't get where I am by thinking about it or dreaming it, got there by doing it.

*Estee Lauder*

Excellence means doing the little things well.

*Buck Rogers*

You get up, you suit up, and you show up; you work smarter than you ever have before.

*Mary Frances Burleson*

The Lord provides for those who wait on Him, but, in the meantime, you'd better work you're a_ _ off!

*Cleada Smith*

You get the best out of others when you get the best out of yourself.

*Harvey Firestone*

I'm a great believer in hard work if you want to be successful. Practice gives you command of what you already have in your mind.

*Les Paul*

Well done is better than well said.

*Poor Richard*

No matter how well I was doing, I always felt I could do a little bit more by going out and doing extra work.

*Rod Carew*

You harvest what you plant, whether good or bad.

*Proverbs 14:14*

If you are too lazy to plow, don't expect a harvest.

*Proverbs 20:4*

I don't care if I was a ditch digger at a dollar a day; I'd want to do my job better than the fellow next to me. I'd want to be the best at whatever I do.

*Branch Rickey*

The key is to keep working. How many people do you know who talk about retiring, but when they do, they start complaining about how boring it is to play golf every day. I may not always like the work I get, but it keeps me going.

*Ernest Borgnine*

Pray as if everything depends on God. Work as if everything depends on you.

*John Wesley*

I like what I'm doing up here. I know what I'm doing up here. I want to keep doing it as long as I'm strong enough to know that I'm doing it right.

*Ralph Hall*

The more you learn the more you earn.

*Robert Dedman*

Fine-tuning work habits, is like focusing through a pair of binoculars: a small adjustment at the source makes yards of difference off in the distance. Slight improvements in daily work routines make a tremendous difference in the eventual results. Doing the really relevant things doesn't just improve business slightly; working a little more and a little smarter will make your business grow disproportionately larger over periods of time.

*Don Hodges*

Be a master of the job before you. Be a student of the job above you. And be a teacher of the job below you.

*Adelfa Callejo*

All growth depends on activity. There is no development physically or intellectually without effort, and effort means work.

*Calvin Coolidge*

If you have to cheat to win, you didn't win.

*Otto Mangold*

If I believe in something, I sell it and sell it hard.

*Estee Lauder*

There are no traffic jams in the extra mile.

*Roger Staubach*

Doing the best at this moment puts you in the best place for the next moment.

*Oprah Winfrey*

A CEO shouldn't leave until quitting time, just like everyone else. If he makes the biggest bucks, he ought to put in the longest hours. As for limousines and corporate planes, I've got nothing against them as long as they are used as tools, not rewards. I use the company airplane. It's fast and efficient, and there have been times when it has made the difference between making a deal and not making it.

*Boone Pickens*

What success I achieved in the theater is due to the fact that I always worked just as hard when there were ten people in the house as when there were thousands – just as hard in Springfield IL as on Broadway.

*Bill "Bojangles" Robinson*

There's just one way to achieve true job security: stand ready to reinvent yourself – no matter what your age, your education, your skill set, or the color of your collar – sometimes more than once.

*Douglas Warshaw*

In order to be successful, you must have principles and discipline. You can't be successful if you don't have the discipline.

Preparation is the most important thing, in everything really. Because it is how well you prepare that will determine your confidence level. What also makes a difference is not just saying what you're going to do, but rather visualizing it actually happening.

Victory is not out of your control. You prepare yourself for victory, you think and plan and train and sweat and work as hard as you can to reach you goal. And you go out and perform at your absolute best because that's the only way to play. You will not win without that.

Happiness is a by-product. You must be enjoying what you are doing in life, not trying to do something to enjoy life. I play because I enjoy playing. I play for fun. I try to learn from every game. I try to improve and do better. It's the journey, not the destination, that matters.

*Hakeem Olajuwon*

Freedom is paramount, but not without our integrity.

*Charlie Plum*

I had three rules for my players: No profanity. Don't criticize a teammate. Never be late.

*John Wooden*

Give me a choice between an outstanding athlete with poor character and a lesser athlete with good character, and I'll choose the latter every time.

*Tom Landry*

You will have nothing in this life without the respect and trust of your friends and family.

*Camille Hodges Hays*

**Horse Sense. Street Smarts.**

# Success

**Tim Cox,** *More Than Just a Horse*

What is success? Ask ten different people and get ten different answers. Success is very personal. It is achieving or being on the road to achieving a dream. At one extreme, it may be surviving. It may be achieving something you desire. It may be helping someone else realize their potential or overcoming some obstacle. We know success when we feel it deep within our being.

Failing to prepare is preparing to fail.

*John Wooden*

If we never make mistakes, then we are most likely not being very innovative and not taking enough risks.

*William Wrigley, Jr.*

I firmly believe that the winners are separated from the losers mainly by their desire to exceed.

*Earl Anthony*

To group and hold a vision, that is the very essence of successful leadership.

*Ronald Reagan*

Expect to make mistakes. Nothing important will be accomplished if you make only safe decisions.

*Warren Buffett*

The way to succeed is to double your failure rate.

*Thomas Watson*

Success is the scariest time of all.

*Kenneth H. Olsen*

There's no such thing as accomplishment; it's overcoming obstacles.

*Anonymous*

Excellence can be attained if you care more than others think is wise, risk more than others think is safe, dream more than others think is practical and expect more than others think is possible.

*Napoleon Hill*

Focus on what people can do, not what they can't.

*Peter Drucker*

Don't let failure get you down and don't let success go to your head.

*Ken Zschappel*

I don't think any successful businessman started out saying, 'I'm going to make a million bucks.' He got excited about an idea. He had a dream. He loved the process. You have to love what you're doing.

*Robert Pritikin*

Success is never final.

*J.W. Marriott*

Failing is not a sign of no talent—it is participating in the crucible of creativity.

*John Bachrus*

Success is like a vitamin.

*Mel Levine, MD*

There is no such thing as a born leader. You are what you perceive yourself to be.

*Gen. Norman Schwarzkopf*

To be the best of the best, you make your mistakes and go on.

Top Gun *(movie)*

The evil man gets rich for the moment, but the good man's reward lasts forever.

*Proverbs 11: 18*

If you are not failing a lot you are probably not being as creative as you could. You are not stretching your imagination enough.

*John Bachrus*

The lessons I had learned within these few months were far more important than the money earned or lost. I became impressed with the maxim that the person with the superior knowledge of the wares, be he buyer or seller, has the decided advantage.

*Dean Krakel*

### Elaine's Eight—Rules for Successful Living

1. Saddle you own horse...never wait. You're in charge of your life and your career.

2. Like what you do, look for the positives in every situation. Play the hand you're dealt.

3. Turn on a dime, changes will just keep coming.

4. Stay connected...develop and nurture relationships.

5. Practice free speech...communicate all the time.

6. Get over it...don't dwell on the past.

7. Develop your funny bone...lighten up, loosen up and laugh.

8. Strengthen your backbone...do the right thing when it's not easy or popular.

*Elaine Agather*

What kind of man would live where there is no danger? I don't believe in taking foolish chances. Nothing can be accomplished by not taking any chances at all.

*Charles A. Lindbergh*

Two roads diverged in a wood, and I—
I took the one less traveled by,
and that has made all the difference.

*Robert Frost*

If customers are happy, the business will flourish.

*John P. Mackey*

Being treated with respect is something every employee deserves, regardless of rank. Not only is it right, it has a positive effect on a company's overall success.

*Mary Kay Ash*

Being successful in business isn't a matter of taking advantage of people who need your product and services. On the contrary, it's a matter of giving them so much value, care, and attention, they would feel guilty even thinking about doing business with somebody else.

*Mary Kay Ash*

I realized my own limitations. I conceded that it was impossible to succeed solely on skill, on emotion, even on determination. Any success I ever attained would require the utmost in preparation and knowledge.

*Tom Landry*

Too many people in life spend too much time keeping score, so it's impossible for them to play the game. While it's important to master details, you shouldn't lose sight of the big picture.

*Mark Spitz*

Success breeds success. After awhile, one gets self-assured after demonstrating he can do things as well as or better than anyone else.

*Dr. Denton Cooley*

Success is the scariest time of all.

*Kenneth Olsen*

I attribute the little I know to my not having been ashamed to ask for information...and to my rule of conversing with all descriptions of men on those topics that form their own peculiar professions and pursuits.

*John Locke*

The formula for success is simple: practice and concentration, then more practice and concentration.

*Babe Didrikson Zaharias*

To laugh often and much, to win the respect of intelligent people and affection of children; to earn the appreciation of honest critics and endure the betrayal of false friends; to appreciate beauty, to find the best in others, to leave the world a bit better, whether by a healthy child, a garden patch or a redeemed social condition; to know even one life has breathed easier because you have lived—this is to have succeeded.

*Ralph Waldo Emerson*

The world doesn't stop when you lose. You must think about the good things that happened to you. You must look ahead. The only way a person can really become strong is to have setbacks.

*Tom Landry*

As a rule, he or she who has the most information will have the greatest successes in life.

*Benjamin Disraeli*

The way to succeed is to double your failure rate.

*Thomas Watson*

A leader has to establish trust—be believable. He must be known as one striving for excellence. They must feel that he cares for them.

*Lou Holtz*

You have to keep asking yourself, 'how can I improve, how can I make it better?' Don't just say 'how can I make more money?' That is the wrong reason. You have to have passion for what you do. Having interest isn't good enough. If people only have an interest, they won't spend the time. If you really want to spend the time, you have to think how you can make your business more successful. To take it from good to great, you must pay attention to details.

*Wolfgang Puck*

We must not let success breed complacency, cockiness, greediness, laziness, indifference, preoccupation with nonessentials, bureaucracy, hierarchy, quarrelsomeness, or obliviousness to threats posed by the outside world. A company is never more vulnerable than when it is at the height of its success.

*Herb Kelleher*

Don't be afraid of failing or feel guilty for not understanding something. Look things up and try to make them understandable.

*Middleton J. Jameson*

Success and risk, you can't have one without the other. Success comes to people who are willing to let it all hang out there.

*Mike Egan*

All work is work for a team. No individual has the temperament and skills to do the job. The purpose of a team is to make strengths productive and weaknesses irrelevant.

*Peter Drucker*

The good man's earnings advance the cause of righteousness. The evil man squanders his on sin.

*Proverbs 10:16*

When you're in grammar school, high school, even college, what you're judged on is your ability to answer the questions other people ask of you. I want to encourage students to go in the other direction that is to ask great questions themselves. I think the hallmark of people who've often been very successful is the quality of the questions they ask.

*Robert Langer*

I do not know of anyone who has gotten to the top without hard work. That is the recipe. It will not always get your to the top but should get you pretty near.

*Margaret Thatcher*

Most people don't take risk because they are afraid to fail, to embarrass themselves.

*Ed Werkenmayer*

I learned early on that you play by the rules. It's no fun if you cheat to win.

*Boone Pickens*

You can make more friends in two months by becoming interested in other people than you can in two years by trying to get other people interested in you.

*Dale Carnegie*

Champions aren't made in gyms. Champions are made from something they have deep inside them—a desire, a dream, a vision. They have to have the skill, and the will. But the will must be stronger than the skill.

*Muhammad Ali*

I really believe that success in business comes from doing the right thing.

*Howard Schultz*

If I have a meeting that ends with an action item, I do it immediately. If I have mail to send, I do it right away. I find when you do that, your life becomes just managing the day.

*Nandan Nilekani*

I think the most important single thing in people's success is whether they are lucky enough to be able to earn their living doing something that, if they could afford to, they would do without pay.

*Milton Friedman*

I think the most unlucky people in the world are those who have to earn their living by doing something in which they would not voluntarily work overtime.

*Milton Friedman*

Success is not going to come from just wishing for it. It comes from determination and hard work. You've got to prepare yourself.

*Marques Haynes*

If a man is working toward a predetermined goal and knows where he's going, that man is a success. If he's not doing that he's a failure.

*Earl Nightingale*

Success isn't about knowing what to do. Success is about doing it. All of the knowledge in the world about gap zapping—even having perfect access to perfect mentors—doesn't account for squat unless you do something about it.

*Sheldon Boules*

Success is going from failure to failure without losing enthusiasm.

*Winston Churchill*

If you do a little more than your competition, you'll stand head and shoulders above them.

*Ed Moore*

The most appealing thing about being an entrepreneur has to be the thrill of the action and the win at the end of the day, knowing as an entrepreneur that you're not going to win every time. You also know, as an entrepreneur, that you're putting your money at risk, your reputation at risk, and you're working your butt off. That's the way the game goes. You put two or three wins together, and your start thinking you're real smart. Then you miss a couple of times, and you realize that you aren't as smart as you thought you were.

*Boone Pickens*

If you find a good solution and become attached to it, the solution may become your next problem.

*Dr. Robert Anthony*

The secret of my success was that somehow I always managed to live to fly another day.

*Chuck Yeager*

Take a method and try it. If it fails, admit it frankly and try another. But above all, try something.

*Franklin Roosevelt*

Failure in life cannot happen unless it has your permission.

*John Hagee*

Continuous effort, not strength or intelligence, is the key to unlock your potential

*Winston Churchill*

You can't be a success in any business without believing that it is the greatest business in the world. You have to put your heart in the business and the business in your heart.

*Thomas Watson, Sr.*

You're not going to get promoted to a better job until you're over-qualified for what you now do.

*John Hagee*

The difference between winning and losing is quitting.

*Ross Perot*

I've learned that so much success comes from taking negatives and turning them into positives.

*Norm Pattiz*

A successful person is someone who does what he knows he should do even when he doesn't feel like doing it.

*Robert Jeffress*

We sometimes learn a lot from our failures if we have put into the effort the best thought and work we are capable of.

*Thomas Edison*

Plans fail for lack of counsel, but with many advisors they succeed.

*Proverbs 15:22*

Visualize yourself doing things correctly and being successful: put we before me and define your success within your team's success.

*Jamaal Wilkes*

Winning is the only thing, no 'I' in team.

*Wes Windmiller*

It is impossible to live without failing at something, unless you live so cautiously that you might as well not have lived at all—in which case, you fail by default.

*J.K. Rowling*

When I talk about our culture and what's required to be successful, it includes love of the business and the passion and energy to be the best. You have to be honest to create the trust to be the best, and you have to have a sense of humor to keep the perspective to be the best.

*John Dooner*

Long-range goals keep you from being frustrated by short term failures.

*J.C. Penney*

I don't ever go into anything giving myself an excuse not to succeed, and it has worked out for me. I'm always willing to sacrifice whatever it takes to be successful, and if I've done everything and I don't have success, I can live with that.

*Kurt Warner*

A leader is someone who stands out in front of his men, but he doesn't get too far out where he cannot hear their footsteps. If he's too far away, he's not being a leader.

*Tommy Lasorda*

Failure is okay. It's what you learn and how you rebound that's important.

*Rebecca Ramos*

Don't waste your time looking for shortcuts to success. There aren't any. Do the right things week after week, month after month, and year after year, and you will prevail.

*Don Connelly*

The motivation must come from within.

*Earl Woods*

If you want to move your career forward and find success, you have to move yourself out of your comfort zone.

*Harry Markopolos*

The big difference between those who are successful and those who are not is that successful people learn from their mistakes and the mistakes of others.

*Sir John Templeton*

I was searching for the answer for so long, and the answer was right in front of me. Do what I do best.

*Tommy Hilfiger*

Originality and success are strangers to one another, but I also hold that originality, despite appearances, will end by making itself felt, and that easy success is soon forgotten.

*Jean Renoir*

Go straight ahead. Do what you want to do. Do it well.

*Liza Minnelli*

A fool with a plan is better than a genius without a plan.

*Boone Pickens*

Success is the child of audacity.

*Benjamin Disraeli*

One thing I've learned is to play to your strengths and don't overreact to the next emerging opportunity. If you understand why you're distinct and you focus on that, your chances of succeeding go up dramatically.

*Ted Fernandez*

I never heard of someone stumbling on something sitting down.

*Charles Kettering*

Where you get to the point you don't have to make a deal, you might make a good one.

*D. D. Harrington*

If you have a good idea, don't let anyone talk you out of it.

*Leonard Lauder*

Don't quit at age 65—that's the time to begin.'

*Col. Harlan Sanders*

Success is built on small margins.

*Herman Pistor*

Failing is good. If you never fail, you'll never be wildly innovative.

*Jennifer Pritchard*

Confidence is something rooted in the unpleasant, harsh aspects of life. The longer you are able to survive and succeed, the better you are able to survive and succeed.

*An Wang*

In order to succeed, we have to fail over and over again. All the words in the world cannot prepare us for that. We get rejected constantly and we never really know why. Anticipating rejection is as discouraging as the rejection itself. That's precisely why three out of every four who have to prospect in order to make a living fear prospecting. And the stepchild of fear is procrastination. 'I'll prospect tomorrow. I've got lots of other stuff to do today.' Adios, career!

*Don Connelly*

If you do something really interesting, it's likely to be successful. And if it's not successful, at least it was interesting while you were doing it.

*Jimmy Wales*

Success is family, friends, and the ability to pay the bills.

*George Lundeen*

Be always sure you are right, then go ahead.

*Davy Crockett*

There is the will to conquer, the impulse to fight, to prove oneself superior to others, to succeed for the sake, not of the fruits of success, but of success itself. There is the joy of creating, of getting things done, or simply exercising one's energy and ingenuity.

*Wall Street Journal*

The most successful business leaders often have many failures, large and small, along the way. The difference is that they learn as much from failure as they do from success. Another lesson is that the future belongs to risk takers who sense opportunities when others see only folly or danger.

*Wall Street Journal*

Remember to plant trees under whose branch you will never sit, but when you are gone, people will remember you were here.

*John Hagee*

An award is for what you did yesterday. It's what you are doing today and what you plan to do tomorrow that counts.

*Dan Beck*

Honesty is the best policy.

*Stan Hays*

Most great ideas are inspired by the good ideas of others.

*Eric J. Marshall*

# Perseverance

**Tim Cox,** *Reflections of a Passing Day*

Perseverance is going ahead and trying when everything, except that inner voice, says stop. It's determination. It's faith in yourself. It's the reward at the end of the trip. It's a vision that says "come on, you can do it!" It may even be a response to "your calling."

The difference between winning and losing is quitting.

*Ross Perot*

You can't do anything until you try.

*Oliver Hodges*

Accept your failures as learning opportunities and don't be afraid to try again. If something other than what you anticipated or desired happens, if it doesn't work out, know that you can accept failure without being personally defeated. The secret of the Joy of Failure is that you can make a stepping-stone out of a stumbling block, if you approach it with a positive attitude. You can handle an event that doesn't work out and still go on and try something else. What you cannot permit is a paralysis that keeps you from trying anything. This paralysis is more dangerous than any number of failures. If you are frozen stiff by fear, you try nothing, and that is what you produce. Success belongs to the brave soul who is willing to try for the 422nd time.

*James Williams Robbins*

No man in the wrong can stand up against a fellow that's in the right and keeps on a coming.

*Capt. W. J. McDonald*

The useful man never leads the easy, sheltered, knockless, unshocked life. If he is worthwhile, he has passed through a series of hard knocks.

*Thomas Edison*

It ain't over till it's over.

*Yogi Berra*

A new idea either finds a champion or it dies. Champions of new ideas must display persistence and courage of heroic quality.

*Paul Eisenstein*

You miss 100% of the shots you don't take.

*Wayne Gretzky*

To see a seed flower, it has to be planted. If you are content with planting radish seeds, you'll get radishes in a few weeks. When you start planting acorns, the full-fledged oak may take years.

*Conrad Hilton*

There is no such thing as accomplishment; it's overcoming obstacles.

*Anonymous*

It is not only by yielding to one's impulses that one achieves greatness, but also by patiently filing away the steel wall that separates what one feels from what one is capable of doing.

*Vincent van Gogh*

An inventor fails 999 times and if he succeeds once, he's in. He treats his failures simply as practice shots.

*Charles Kettering*

Do not be too timid and squeamish about your actions. The more experiments you make the better. What if they are a little coarse and you may get your coat soiled or torn? What if you do fail and get fairly rolled in the dirt once or twice? Up again; you shall never be so afraid of the tumble.

*Ralph Waldo Emerson*

I try to skate to where the puck is going to be, not where it is at the moment.

*Wayne Gretzky*

If you really want to get something done, start on it, keep at it, and it will eventually happen.

*Dick Goodwin*

Don't fear failure, and don't crave success. Don't worry about whether an invention is going to be successful or not, or if it's going to make money or not. Just keep at it. The true reward is not in the results; it is in the doing.

*Wilson Greatbatch*

Sticking is one of the big things in salesmanship. Nearly all buyers say, 'No!' at first. Real salesman stick until the buyer has used his last No!

*William Wrigley, Jr.*

The manner in which one endures what must be endured is more important than the thing that must be endured.

*Dean Acheson*

When one door closes, another door opens.

*Helen Keller*

It is a mistake to look too far ahead. Only one link in the chain of destiny can be handled at a time.

*Winston Churchill*

Life is like a shark. You have to continue to move forward and do things better every day, or you die.

*Larry Ellison*

Watching the best is a great way to learn. I observed and emulated their expertise. I learned that if you do have a disappointment or failure, you have to keep working, keep it in the back of your mind.

*Dr. Denton Cooley*

Refuse to throw in the towel. Go that extra mile that failures refuse to travel. The definition of successful people is simply ordinary people with extraordinary determination.

*Mary Kay Ash*

**Horse Sense. Street Smarts.**

That which we persist in doing becomes easier for us to do; not that the nature itself is changed, but our power to do it is increased.

*Albert Einstein*

Nothing in the world can take the place of persistence. Talent will not; nothing is more common than unsuccessful men with talent. Genius will not; unrewarded genius is almost a proverb. Education will not; the world is full of educated derelicts. Persistence and determination are omnipotent. The slogan 'press on' has solved and always will solve the problems of the human race.

*Calvin Coolidge*

I trained myself that if something goes wrong you just wash it out of your head and keep thinking positively.

*Peggy Fleming*

Continuing to learn is crucial to any pursuit. You'd better do that or you're going to be left behind. It's important to learn new methods. Someone who's unencumbered by past practices may produce an improved solution. Many people consider what they've learned in school and during their careers to be frozen in space, but that's dangerous thinking. Because once you've learned something can't be done, you're less likely to test that belief. The other guy, who doesn't know that it can't be done because he never had that experience, simply goes ahead and it turns out that, yes, it can be done.

*Robert Adler*

When you take a risk sometimes you lose, but sometimes it pays off big.

*Ewing M. Kauffman*

Each setback prepared me for a greater triumph. I've always believed that you can be positive just as well as you can think negative.

*Sugar Ray Robinson*

Adversity in my life proved to be an advantage. It gave me an acceptance of change and a sense of confidence that I can make it through any of the challenges that life may give. At a very early age, I learned that hard work and persistence would payoff whether on the playing field, in the classroom, or in my career.

*Jim Keyes*

One of the responses to crises is entrepreneurship. It's sort of like a forest fire; the ashes of the catastrophe are the fertilizer of the next growth.

*David Birch*

Somebody said it couldn't be done. But he, with a chuckle, replied, maybe it couldn't, but he would be one who wouldn't say so till he tried. So he buckled right in with a bit of a grin on his face; if he doubted, he hid it. He started to sigh as he tackled the thing that couldn't be done and he did it.

*Edward A. Guest*

In his book, How to Beat Wall Street, Myron Kondel recounts a classic article on Ted Williams, where Williams said that the record of which he was most proud was most bases on balls. Williams said it proved he had the patience and discipline to wait for the pitch he wanted before he swung.

I've missed more than 9,000 shots in my career. I've lost almost 300 games. Twenty-six times, I've been trusted to take the game winning shot and missed. I've failed over and over and over again in my life. And that is why I succeed.

*Michael Jordan*

One oil well doesn't make an oilfield. One victory doesn't take care of the whole situation. I've always believed that whatever success you had would be a series of small victories and that you could never predict when you are going to get a home run. By getting up to bat a lot, you increase your odds to get a home run, so you try to do that. The more opportunities you have to get up to bat, the more opportunities you have to be successful.

*T. Boone Pickens*

**Horse Sense. Street Smarts.**

Babe Ruth struck out 1,330 times, but he also hit 714 home runs!
Practice equals spontaneity.

*Billie Jean King*

"Not everything is going to work out the first time or the second
time or even the third time. You just have to step back and ask yourself why this didn't work out and what do I have to do differently.

*Lou Holtz*

A person who cannot face a fear will always be running from it...
never take the counsel of your fears and proceed aggressively. The
courageous man is the man who forces himself, in spite of his fear,
to carry on.

*Gen. George Patton*

A lot of times winners are just those who are still around after everyone else gives up.

*Mark McCormack*

If you're not willing to take a risk and make mistakes, you'll never do
anything right.

*Sandy Weill*

Intense concentration hour after hour can bring out responses they
didn't know they had.

*Edwin Land*

Courage is being scared to death but saddling up anyway.

*John Wayne*

The only thing that is necessary for liberty to perish is for good men
to do nothing.

*Sir Edmund Burke*

The real world, whether in business or government, requires that you don't jump to the endgame or to success right away. You do it piece by piece. Some people get immobilized when they come to a roadblock. My answer is, 'you know, it's a shame it's there, but now where else can we go? Let's just do it. '

*Michael Bloomberg*

Persist eternally.

*Matt Chambers*

It requires courage to begin something, perseverance to see it through.

*Robert Jeffress*

Never give up; never give up, never, never, never give up.

*Winston Churchill*

If there's no struggle, there's no progress.

*Frederick Douglass*

Willpower is the willingness to indulge yourself and be willing to do what is necessary to accomplish what you want.

*Bill Russell*

You're more valuable because of the experiences you've been through that were failures.

*Gordon Moore*

In times of uncertainty, we can give up, give in or give out. However, through the power of God's leadership, we must reach up, seeking his guidance. We must reach in to fine tune our processes and make the most of the resources we have.

*O.S. Hawkins*

Though the vision tarries, wait for it; it will surely come.

*Habakkuk 2:30*

Never tell lies or be deceitful in what you say. Keep looking straight ahead, without turning aside. Know where you are headed, and you will stay on solid ground.

*Proverbs 4:24-26*

Most of the important things in the world have been accomplished by people who have kept on trying when there seemed to be no hope at all.

*Dale Carnegie*

When all the world is surfaced over with concrete, one day a blade of grass will spring up.

*Ilya Ehrenburg*

Pain is temporary. Quitting lasts forever.

*Lance Armstrong*

Intelligent investors act out of patience and courage, not panic.

*Jason Zweig*

I made it on my own, having the good luck to be born in America, where starting with nothing doesn't mean you have to end up that way.

*Boone Pickens*

The man who can drive himself farther once the effort gets painful is the man who will win.

*Roger Bannister*

We all have an Everest, and you have to do what it takes to get to the top.

*Andrea Cardona*

In some ways you don't become a winner until you fail.

*Mark Sanford*

When you get into a tight place...till it seems as though you could not hang on a minute longer, never give up then, for that is just the place and time that the tide will turn.

*Harriet Beecher Stowe*

### The Man in the Arena

It is not the critic who counts; not the man who points out how the strong man stumbles, or where the doer of deeds could have done them better. The credit belongs to the man who is actually in the arena, whose face is marred by dust and sweat and blood, who strives valiantly, who errs, who comes short again and again, because there is no effort without error and shortcoming; but who does actually strive to do the deeds; who knows great enthusiasms, the great devotions; who spends himself in a worthy cause; who at the best knows in the end the triumph of high achievement, and who at the worst, if he fails, at least fails while daring greatly, so that his place shall never be with those cold and timid souls who neither know victory nor defeat.

*Theodore Roosevelt*

Everything we do is driven by seeing opportunity rather than being worried about defending.

*Jeff Bezos*

# Index

## A

## B

# C

**Horse Sense. Street Smarts.**

**Horse Sense. Street Smarts.**

**Index**      211

**Horse Sense. Street Smarts.**

**Horse Sense. Street Smarts.**

# S

**Horse Sense. Street Smarts.**

**Horse Sense. Street Smarts.**